Bilingual–Bicultural Education

Octavio A. Ballesteros

Bilingual–Bicultural Education
An Annotated Bibliography 1936–1982

McFarland & Company, Inc.,
Publishers
Jefferson, North Carolina, and London
1983

Octavio A. Ballesteros, born in San Antonio, Texas, has a doctorate in education from East Texas State University. He has directed bilingual education at the college and school level and has been a school principal and university professor, journal editor and writer. Dr. Ballesteros has written other books, including *Preparing Teachers for Bilingual Education* (1979), *Mexican Proverbs: The Philosophy, Wisdom and Humor of a People* (1979), and *Behind Jail Bars* (1979).

Library of Congress Cataloguing-in-Publication Data

Ballesteros, Octavio A., 1936–
   Bilingual–bicultural education.

   Bibliography: p.
   Includes index.
   1. Education, Bilingual – United States – Bibliography.
2. Intercultural education – United States – Bibliography.
I. Title.
Z5815.U5B34 1983   [LC3719]   016.37197   83-42884

ISBN 0-89950-077-3 (pbk.)

Manufactured in the United States of America

McFarland & Company, Inc., Publishers
  Box 611, Jefferson, North Carolina 28640

This book is dedicated to the teachers
in the United States who are teaching
in a bilingual classroom

TABLE OF CONTENTS

INTRODUCTION

Bilingual education is the use of two languages as mediums of instruction in a school setting. Bicultural education may be defined as an educational program which provides students of a foreign culture with the opportunity to become knowledgeable in the customs, traditions, history and heritage of their adopted culture.

When bilingual education is combined with bicultural education, a comprehensive education program results, which may be called bilingual-bicultural education--an education program which includes a second language and culture in the school curriculum. The end product of a bilingual-bicultural education program is an individual who can communicate in two languages and who can function in two cultures.

There are numerous types of bilingual-bicultural education programs in the United States. A few examples of American bilingual education programs are the English-German, English-French, English-Chinese, English-Navajo, English-Portuguese, English-Vietnamese, and English-Spanish programs. Altogether, forty different languages presently are taught in the various bilingual-bicultural programs in the United States.

The English-Spanish bilingual-bicultural education program currently is the most prevalent form, primarily because of the large influx of Mexicans, Puerto Ricans, Dominicans, Cubans, and other Central and South Americans into this nation in recent years.

The primary purpose of this work is to meet the informational needs of individuals involved in the field of bilingual-bicultural education. It is the author's opinion that this work is the most practical annotated bilingual-bicultural education sourcebook available.

While I was writing my dissertation on bilingual education for the Mexican American student, I began collecting numerous references on bilingual-bicultural education. Even today, I still continue to collect references in this area. In this annotated sourcebook I have attempted to include the best of the hundreds of references collected during the past nine years of research on bilingualism and biculturism.

This book primarily is concerned with the bilingual-bicultural education of the Hispanic American student. There are 556 sources organized into 11 categories. The sources cited herein cover all aspects of American bilingual-bicultural education. Because this kind of education is considered to be a component of multilingual-multicultural education, some sources are included in this work that are multilingual and multicultural in content.

There are thousands of students enrolled in American colleges and universities who are taking courses in bilingual-bicultural education and in multicultural education. This sourcebook can direct these students, many of whom are classroom teachers, to publications that contain basic insights into the bilingual-bicultural and multicultural education of children in American schools.

Any professor or student of bilingual-bicultural education is aware that one of the main problems of being an instructor or student of bilingual-bicultural education is the difficulty in finding books, journal articles, or published

1

speeches and papers about bilingual-bicultural education. This sourcebook solves this problem.

Another problem encountered by professors and students is the arduous task of organizing bilingual-bicultural sources into meaningful and manageable subject categories. This sourcebook also solves this problem.

One special feature of this publication is the introductory paragraphs preceding each of the sections of this work. Another feature of this work is that its content can be used by professors and students in each course offered in a college level bilingual-bicultural education program. A third feature of this work is that the categorization of the 556 references contained herein should prove very beneficial to school administrators, classroom teachers, bilingual education consultants, educational researchers, and scholars who need a convenient source of bilingual-bicultural education materials which can be used to prepare staff development programs, workshop presentations, personal development prescriptions, college course assignments, research projects, technical reports, and scholarly papers. A fourth feature of this book is that each reference is annotated for the reader's convenience.

At the writing of this book, there are 241 institutions of higher education in the United States that offer a bilingual-bicultural education program, while 135 institutions offer a multicultural education program. Some of these institutions offer an undergraduate program in bilingual-bicultural education while other institutions offer a bilingual-bicultural education program at the masters or doctoral level. It is anticipated that the number of colleges and universities offering bilingual-bicultural education and multicultural education programs will greatly increase in the coming years.

The author expresses his appreciation to his wife, María del Carmen, for the encouragement and assistance that she provided while this work was in progress. Without her cooperation, this sourcebook might not have been completed.

I

BILINGUALISM, BICULTURALISM, AND BILINGUAL-BICULTURAL EDUCATION

Bilingualism is the ability of a person to understand and communicate in two languages. A bilingual person need not be equally proficient in both languages to be considered bilingual. Most linguistic authorities are in agreement that bilingualism is a personal asset and that bilingualism does not adversely affect the bilingual person's mental development. Most studies on bilingualism conclusively conclude that a person's cognitive development is enhanced by his bilingualism.

Biculturalism is the ability of a person to function effectively in two cultures. A bicultural person is one who, at will, can shift from one cultural "gear" to another. For instance, a bicultural Mexican American understands and can function in both the American culture and the Mexican culture. Because the Mexican American is bicultural, he or she understands the spirit, values, roles, taboos, mannerisms, ethics, and language of both the United States and Mexico.

Bilingual-bicultural education is an educational system which includes a second language and a second culture in the school curriculum. The end product of bilingual-bicultural education is an individual who can communicate in two languages and who can function in two cultures. As our world becomes more interdependent, the demand for bilingual-bicultural individuals will increase. Numerous school districts in the United States have implemented bilingual-bicultural education programs.

The references in this section will provide the reader with insights into bilingualism, biculturalism, and bilingual-bicultural education.

1. ALEXANDER, David, and Alfonso Nava. The How, What, Where and Why of Bilingual Education: A Concise and Objective Guide for School District Planning. San Francisco: R & E Research Associates, 1977. A technical report for scholars conducting research on bilingual education. The book title conveys the content of the text. Soft cover.

2. ANDERSSON, Theodore. "Bilingual Education and Early Childhood," 1973. ERIC Microfiche, ED 074 868. This report discusses the importance of providing bilingual education to pupils during early childhood.

3. _____. "Bilingual Schooling: A Cross-Disciplinary Approach," 1970. ERIC Microfiche, ED 038 628. The author does an admirable job in this article showing that bilingual education can be effective when an interdisciplinary approach is utilized.

4. _____. "Bilingual Schooling: Oasis or Mirage?" Hispania, Volume 52, No. 1 (March, 1969), pages 69-74. Informative and well-written. Suggested reading for the taxpayer who still has doubts about offering bilingual education to American children.

3

5.   AYALA, Armando A. "Rationale for Early Childhood Bilingual-Bicultural Education," 1971. ERIC Microfiche ED 047 869. The following topics are discussed: (a) cultural conflict, (b) early childhood education, (c) English-dominant students, (d) speaking Spanish in the classroom, (e) English as a second language, and (f) types of bilingual programs.

6.   BENDERLY, Beryl L. "The Multilingual Mind," Psychology Today, Volume 15 (March 1981), pages 9-12. The author discusses language, monolingualism, bilingualism, neurology and how the human brain is affected by bilingualism and multilingualism.

7.   BEVERIDGE, John. "Bilingual Programs: Some Doubts and Comments," The Clearing House, Volume 55, No. 5 (January 1982), pages 214-217. The author, a lawyer, discusses the problems faced by bilingual education in the United States. The reasons for opposition to American bilingual education also are mentioned.

8.   "Bilingualism as a Door, Not a Wall," no author. America, Volume 142 (June 7, 1980), pages 472-473. The point is made that Hispanic Americans are in an ideal position to become America's models of the citizens of the future who are better educated than most monolingual citizens because they are bilingual.

9.   DIEBOLD, Richard. "The Consequence of Early Bilingualism on Cognitive Development and Personality Formation," 1966. ERIC Microfiche, ED 020 491. The author deliberates the effects of bilingualism on the personality and mental development of children. This is a subject which should be of interest to educators involved in the dual language development of children.

10.   EARLE, Jane. "Se Habla Español: The Story of the Chicano Education Project," Today's Education, Volume 66 (November-December 1977), pages 76-77. The author describes Colorado's Bilingual Education Act and the state's Chicano Education Project.

11.   EHRLICH, Alan. "Bilingual Teaching and Beginning School Success," 1971, ERIC Microfiche, ED 077 279. The effect bilingual education has on initial school achievement is the main concern of the author in this publication.

12.   FISHMAN, Joshua. "Bilingualism, Intelligence, and Language Learning," The Modern Language Journal, Volume 49, No. 4 (April 1965). The author comments on the effect of being bilingual on an individual's mental prowess and language development. This article should be required reading for all bilingual education majors.

13.   _____. "The Status and Prospects of Bilingualism in the United States," The Modern Language Journal, Volume 49 (1965), pages 143-155. Some American educators maintain -- and perhaps secretly hope -- that bilingualism and bilingual education will somehow "go away." On the other hand many individuals are convinced that bilingualism and bilingual education are "here to stay." This article should appeal to educators who want to determine if bilingualism is a fad or a fixture in our society.

14.   _____, and Robert Cooper. Bilingualism in the Barrio. Bloomington, Indiana: Indiana University Publications, 1971. This publication was written by two nationally recognized experts on bilingualism. Persons interested in learning more about the Mexican American's Spanish dialect will will want to refer to this work.

15. FOSTER, Charles R. "Defusing the Issues in Bilingualism and Bilingual Education," Phi Delta Kappan, Volume 63, No. 5 (January 1982), pages 342-344. This is an article for the person who wishes to obtain an overview of American bilingual education and why bilingual education is plagued with so many problems and detractors in the United States. The author contends that one reason that American bilingual education is so complex is because it must serve the educational and linguistic needs of six major student groups with varying linguistic competence in one or two languages.

16. GAARDER, A. B. "Bilingual Education: Central Questions and Concerns," New York University Education Quarterly, Volume 6, (Summer 1975), page 2. Recommended reading for the person who is not familiar with the rationale of American bilingual education.

17. GATES, Judith Rae. "The Bilingually Advantaged," Todays Education, Volume 59 (December 1970), pages 38-40, 56. While some teachers of Hispanic students seem to believe that bilingualism is a personal disadvantage, most experts in bilingualism agree that the bilingual student has an advantage that most teachers are unprepared to cultivate. An inspiring article.

18. GÓMEZ, Severo. "Bilingual Education in Texas." Educational Leadership, Volume 28 (April 1971), pages 757, 759, 761. The author is the Assistant Commissioner of Education in Texas and an authority on bilingual-bicultural education. An important journal article.

19. HARO, Robert P. "Bicultural and Bilingual Americans: A Need for Understanding," Library Trends, Volume 20 (October 1971), pages 256-270. A scholarly article which will assist teachers in becoming more aware of the unique cultures and languages of America's bicultural and bilingual students. Highly recommended reading. A lengthy article which contains numerous concepts concerning our nation's bicultural-bilingual citizens.

20. HERBERT, Robert K. "Cerebral Asymmetry in Bilinguals and the Deaf: Perspectives on a Common Pattern," Journal of Multilingual and Multicultural Development, Volume 3, No. 1 (1982), pages 47-59. The author discusses the neurolinguistic aspects of bilingualism. Mentioned are some cerebral parallels between deaf persons and some bilinguals.

21. HILL, H. S. "The Effects of Bilingualism on the measured Intelligence of Elementary School Children of Italian Parentage," Journal of Experimental Education, Volume 5 (1936) pages 75-79. The conclusions in this article should prove interesting to teachers of Mexican American students, even though Italian American students' bilingualism is the primary topic discussed by the author.

22. HORNBY, Peter A. (editor). Bilingualism: Psychological, Social and Educational Implications. New York: Academic Press, 1977. The effects of speaking two languages in our society are treated. One of the better collections on bilingualism.

23. JENSEN, J. Vernon. "Bilingualism and Creativity," 1966. ERIC Microfiche, ED 021 848. Are bilingual children more creative than monolingual children? Does bilingualism stimulate the child's imagination? This publication gives the reader an insight into the relationship between creativity and the ability to speak two languages.

24. _____. "Effects of Childhood Bilingualism," Elementary English, Volume

39 (1962), pages 132-143, 358-366. Does a child profit from being bilingual or does speaking two languages adversely affect a child? The author addresses himself to this and related questions in his informative article.

25. JOHN, Vera P. , and Vivian M. Horner. Early Childhood Bilingual Education. New York: MLA, 1971. Most linguistics experts contend that children who are exposed to bilingual education at an early age tend to profit significantly from this form of education. Head start teachers will want to refer frequently to this outstanding publication on early childhood bilingual education.

26. JONES, W. R. "A Critical Study of Bilingualism and Nonverbal Intelligence, " British Journal of Educational Psychology, Volume 30 (1960), pages 71-77. A scholarly study on the effects of speaking two languages on a person's mental prowess. Recommended reading for the serious student of bilingual education.

27. KILPATRICK, James J. "Of Bilingualism and Common Ties, " Nation's Business, Volume 68, No. 10 (October 1980), page 17. The author contends that it would be a great mistake to encourage bilingualism in the United States as a continuing public policy.

28. KOBRICK, Jeffrey W. "The Compelling Case for Bilingual Education, " Saturday Review, Volume 55 (April 29, 1972), pages 54-58. This classic article gives the reader a sound rationale for providing Hispanic students with bilingual education. Operational bilingual education programs are described.

29. KREAR, Serafina E. "The Role of the Mother Tongue at Home and at School in the Development of Bilingualism, " English Language Teaching, Volume 24 (October 1969), pages 2-4. The author makes the point that a bipolar attitude exists in the United States concerning bilingual ability. Bilingualism frequently is prized in language scholars but disdained in native speakers who represent other cultures and different ways of perceiving life.

30. LAMBERT, Wallace E. "A Social Psychology of Bilingualism, " The Journal of Social Issues, Volume 23, No. 2 (April 1967), pages 91-110. In this lengthy article, the author, an authority on bilingualism, discusses the social and psychological implications of being a bilingual person.

31. _____. "Bilingualism and Retardation, " Elementary English, Volume 33 (May 1956), pages 303-304. The author explores the relationship between educational retardation and the ability to communicate in two languages.

32. _____, and Elizabeth Peal. "The Relation of Bilingualism to Intelligence, " in Chapter 10, Language, Psychology, and Culture. Stanford: Stanford University Press, 1972. Do some bilingual students score low on intelligence tests because they are bilingual or because they belong to a culture of poverty? Can bilingualism be an asset to the intellectual development of students? These and related questions are answered in this book chapter.

33. LANDRY, Richard. "Bilingualism and Creative Abilities, " 1969. ERIC Microfiche, ED 039 602. Does bilingualism have a positive effect on the creative abilities of children? Many educators tend to believe that the ability to speak two languages often is a stimulus to children's creative talents. Recommended for the researcher collecting data on creativity.

34. LARA-BRAUD, Jorge. "Bilingualism for Texas: Education for Frater-
nity," 1970. ERIC Microfiche, ED 047 072. The state of Texas, which
is known throughout the nation as an ultraconservative state which is con-
trolled politically by Anglo Americans who come mainly from rural areas, might
consider promoting bilingualism to show its spirit of brotherhood toward persons
who are members of non-Anglo American cultural groups. In this publication,
the author discusses how Texans can use bilingualism to foster brotherliness in
their state.

35. LENTON, Thomas H. "Rationale for Bilingual Education in South Texas,"
1972. ERIC Microfiche, ED 068 256. Teachers in South Texas will find
that this publication was written especially for them. The reasons for
providing a bilingual education for children are enumerated and explained.

36. LEVINSON, Sanford. "Bilingualism: A Symposium," The Nation, Volume
228, No. 10 (March 17, 1979), pages 263-266. The point is made at this
symposium that Spanish-speaking Americans want their children to be taught
the Spanish language because they want to preserve a sense of their cultural heritage. Other important points concerning bilingualism also are made by the speakers at this symposium on bilingualism.

37. LEWIS, E. Glyn. Bilingualism and Bilingual Education: A Comparative
Study. Albuquerque: University of New Mexico Press, 1980. This book
contains considerable information on bilingual education in the United
States, multilingualism, and ethnicity. Two interesting essays are (a) "Needs,
Policies, and Programs in Bilingual Education" and (b) "Justifications of Bi-
lingual Education: Rationales and Group Responses."

38. LIEDTKE, W. W., and L. D. Nelson. "Bilingualism and Conservation,"
1968. ERIC Microfiche, ED 030 110. Recommended for the education
major interested in determining how bilingualism affects a student's
mental operations.

39. MACIAS, Reynaldo. "Our State of Schooling," Nuestro, Volume 3, No. 8
(September 1979), pages 37-40. Recommended reading for Anglo American teachers who instruct Hispanic American students.

40. NEY, James W. "Bilingual Education in Sunday School Country," Elementary English, (February 1974), pages 209-214. The author stresses
that students generally blame themselves for the failure which they encounter in culturally and linguistically insensitive schools.

41. OLSTAD, Charles. "Bilingual Education in Three Cultures," 1968. ERIC
Microfiche, ED 027 515. Many proponents of bilingual education claim
that among other things, bilingual education is a "state of mind." By
state of mind, we mean that educators in bilingual education programs have accepted the idea that not all children will profit from the traditional methods of
instruction used in most American schools and that special instructional techniques must be employed if we hope to be successful in motivating and teaching
children from all cultural groups. In this publication, the author describes
bilingual education programs which serve the children of three cultures.

42. ORNSTEIN, Allan C., and D. U. Levine. "Multicultural Education: Trends
and Issues," Childhood Education, Volume 58, No. 4 (March/April 1982),
pages 241-245. Some of the concepts discussed are: (a) differential

instructional approaches, (b) student learning styles, (c) recognition of dialect differences, (d) bilingual/bicultural education, and (e) the melting pot vs. cultural pluralism.

43. ORTEGA, Luis (editor). Introduction to Bilingual Education. New York: Las Americas Publishing Company, 1975. Ortega's introductory bilingual education book is one of the few comprehensive books available on the subject of American bilingual education. The articles in this reader discuss bilingual education as it applies to the various ethnic groups in this nation.

44. OTHEGUY, Ricardo, and Ruth Otto. "'Static Maintenance' in Bilingual Education," Education Digest, Volume 46 (January 1981), pages 23-35. The authors discuss and explain the following terms: (a) transitional bilingual education programs, (b) maintenance bilingual education program, (c) static maintenance, and (d) developmental maintenance.

45. PAULSTON, Christina B. Bilingual Education: Theories and Issues. Rowley, Massachusetts: Newbury House Publishers, 1980. This work describes the three basic types of bilingual education programs available to American school children. The various goals of bilingual education are listed. Length: 90 pages.

46. PEAL, Elizabeth. The Relation of Bilingualism to Intelligence. Washington, D.C.: American Psychological Association, 1962. Does speaking two languages benefit or harm the mental development of individuals? In this publication, Peal addresses herself to this and related questions concerning the relationship between intelligence and bilingualism.

47. PIFER, Alan. "Bilingual Education and the Hispanic Challenge," Education Digest, Volume 46 (November 1980), pages 12-15. The author warns that supporters of bilingual education must be careful of advancing rationals for bilingual education that go beyond the educational purpose of helping children acquire mental skills which allow them to successfully compete in mainstream America.

48. REYES, Vinicio H. Bicultural-Bilingual Education for Latino Students. New York: Arno Press, 1978. This work stresses that a special form of bilingual and bicultural education is needed for American students of Latino or Hispanic decent.

49. RODRIGUEZ, Armando. "Bilingual Education--A Look Ahead," 1969. ERIC Microfiche, ED 030 505. The author lists the reasons for resistance to bilingualism in the United States. Also mentioned is the rationale for bilingual and bicultural education.

50. SPENCER, María Gutiérrez. "BOLD: Bicultural Orientation and Language Development," Paper presented at the National Convention of the American Association of Teachers of Spanish and Portuguese, 1968. ERIC Microfiche, ED 030 342. In this provocative paper, the author contends that educators can safely conclude that the public schools' policy of stamping out the native languages of the Southwest has stunted the intellectual growth of many children whose dominant language is not English.

51. SPOLSKY, Bernard, and Robert L. Cooper (editors). Case Studies in Bilingual Education. Rowley, Massachusetts: Newbury House Publishers, 1978. This book of readings provides the student of bilingual education

with a worldwide perspective of bilingualism and bilingual schooling. Length: 544 pages.

52. _____, and _____. Frontiers of Bilingual Education. Rowley, Massa-
    chusetts: Newbury House Publishers, 1977. This is a book of readings
    about various aspects of bilingual education. This 326 page book can be
used as an introductory textbook for many bilingual-bicultural education courses
at the undergraduate and graduate levels.

53. ST. CLAIR, Robert, and Guadalupe Valdes (editors). Social and Educa-
    tional Issues in Bilingualism and Biculturalism. Washington, D.C.: Uni-
    versity Press of America, 1982. This book of readings discusses such
topics as: (a) socio-political approaches to language, (b) non-standard Spanish,
(c) language switching, (d) conflict societies, and (e) language loyalty.

54. STONE, Marvin. "Meddling in Bilingual Teaching," U.S. News and World
    Report, Volume 89 (September 22, 1980), page 84. The author is critical
    of the strong bureaucratic control which federal officials have on the nation's
local school systems in the area of bilingual education.

55. STUBING, Charles (editor). "Bilingualism," Third Annual Conference of
    the Southwest Council of Foreign Language Teachers, El Paso, Texas,
    November 4-5, 1966. ERIC Microfiche, ED 016 435. Educators who
possess a superficial knowledge of bilingualism but who wish to become more
knowledgeable on the subject will want to refer to this publication. The primary
objective of bilingual education is discussed.

56. "Taking Bilingualism to Task," no author. Time, Volume 119 (April 19,
    1982), page 68. This short article stresses the "inevitable pain" that non-
    English-speaking American children feel when they realize that their home
culture and home language are not part of the monolingual-monocultural school
program. However, the point is made that most American bilingual programs
are delaying the assimilation of non-English-dominant students.

57. TAYLOR, Marie E. "An Overview of Research on Bilingualism," 1970.
    ERIC Microfiche, ED 049 876. Research oriented educators involved in
    bilingual education program development should find value in this compre-
hensive study on American bilingualism. Recommended reading for doctoral
students majoring in bilingual education.

58. TURNER, Paul R. Bilingualism in the Southwest. Tucson: University of
    Arizona Press, 1973. The author's book on Spanish-English bilingualism
    can be used as a textbook in some introductory courses in undergraduate bi-
lingual education. Professors of bilingual education will want Turner's book in
their personal professional library.

59. VALDEZ, Armando. "The Media vs. Bilingual Education," Nuestro, Volume
    3, No. 8 (September 1979), pages 44-46. Does the American media tend to
    support or oppose the bilingual education of children? The author of this
article presents his viewpoint on this educational issue.

60. VALENCIA, Atilano A. "Bilingual Bicultural Education: A Perspective
    Model in Multicultural America," 1969. ERIC Microfiche, ED 028 017.
    This publication contains a clear explanation of the need for bilingual-bi-
cultural education in the United States, a multicultural nation. Many educational
concepts are defined in this publication.

61. VALVERDE, Leonard A. (editor). Bilingual Education for Latinos. Washington, D.C.: Association for Supervisors and Curriculum Development, 1978. This is a book of basic readings for students taking an introductory course in bilingual-bicultural education. Some concepts discussed are: (a) language assessment, (b) language evaluation, (c) curriculum development, (d) community involvement, and (e) staff development. Length: 120 pages.

62. WALKER, Judith. Education in Two Languages: A Guide for Bilingual Teachers. Washington, D.C.: University Press of America, 1979. This 104 page booklet provides a text which may be used in competency-based teacher education courses. Describes the principles of bilingual education in the U.S.A. Soft cover.

63. WALSH, Donald D. "Bilingualism and Bilingual Education: A Guest Editorial," Foreign Language Annals, Volume 2 (March 1969), pages 298-303. Are bilingual education programs effective in developing bilingualism in students? Are there two sides to the issue of providing bilingual education to Hispanic students? This five-page article introduces the layman to some of the important issues in bilingual education.

64. WEST, Michael. "Bilingualism," English Language Teaching, Volume 12 (1958), pages 94-97. West's article provides the reader with some of the fundamental concepts needed to comprehend the many ramifications of being a bilingual person in American society. A scholarly, informative and important article on bilingualism.

65. YAMAMOTO, Kaoru. "Bilingualism: A Brief Review," Mental Hygiene, Volume 48 (1968), pages 468-477. Some concepts discussed in this article are: (a) cultural conflict, (b) language, (c) culture, (d) bilingualism, (e) language acquisition, and (f) social prestige.

66. ZIRKEL, Perry Alan. "Two Languages Spoken Here," Grade Teacher, Volume 88 (April 1971), pages 36-40, 59. A bilingual education program classroom is a place where a child is encouraged to speak two languages--his home language and the English language. Persons who want to be converted to the philosophy of bilingual education should absorb the thoughts in this persuasive article.

II

FIRST LANGUAGE AND
SECOND LANGUAGE TEACHING

A first language may be defined as the language that a monolingual person learned from his parents. In the case of a bilingual person, the first language is his or her stronger language. A first language sometimes is used as a synonym of home language--the language that most frequently is spoken by a person's parents and siblings. A person first learns to think, comprehend, and speak in the home language. Most of the verbal concepts acquired by a child are in his or her home language.

Children, when they first enroll in school, should be taught in their home language (first language). School children in the United States whose first language is not English are at an educational disadvantage when they initially are taught to read and write in English instead of in their stronger language, their first language.

A second language may be defined as the new language a monolingual person is striving to master. In the case of a bilingual person, the second language is his or her weaker language.

Persons who have tried to learn a second language realize that it is no simple feat. Most persons in the United States who have attempted to learn a second language have been unsuccessful in mastering it. Three reasons why many second language learners have failed to master a new language are: (1) the instructional methology used by second language teachers often has been inadequate, (2) American publishers, as a group, have failed to produce effective second language learning textbooks, and (3) second language learners frequently have not been sufficiently motivated to learn a new language.

Second language proficiency is not something that can be obtained easily. Sincere interest, practice and determination are prerequisites for success in mastering a new language.

Most American teachers are proficient in first language instructional methodology but unfortunately, most American teachers are not proficient in second language instructional methodology.

The sources in this section should prove useful to teachers who want to become effective in both first language instructional methodology and second language instructional methodology.

67. ALATIS, James E. English as a Second Language in Bilingual Education. Washington, D.C.: TESOL, 1976. A book of articles pertaining to the role of ESL (English as a second language) in bilingual education. This book provides the reader with a comprehensive look at second language learning and bilingual education.

68. ALLEN, E. D. Classroom Techniques: Foreign Languages and English as a Second Language. New York: Harcourt, Brace & Jovanovich, Inc., 1977. For teachers of non-English-dominant students who want their students to master the English language as rapidly as possible.

69. ALLEN, Harold and Russel N. Campbell. Teaching English as a Second Language: A Book of Readings. New York: McGraw-Hill Book Company, 1972. For the teacher who wants to learn the basics of second language teaching methodology.

70. ARENDT, Jermaine D. , and Dale L. Lange (editors). Foreign Language Learning. Today and Tomorrow. New York: Pergamon Press, 1979. The contributors to this book of readings discuss the future challenges which will be faced by educators involved in foreign language teaching and learning.

71. BARKIN, Florence, and Gail Guntermann. "The Case of Learning Foreign Languages," Today's Education, Volume 71. No. 1 (February-March 1982), pages 48-50, 52. The authors contend that Americans' incompetence in foreign languages no longer can be justified in a changing and interdependent world.

72. BARNITZ, John G. "Orthographies, Bilingualism and Learning to Read English as a Second Language," The Reading Teacher, Volume 35, No. 5 (February 1982), pages 560-567. The author stresses that students who are learning to read a second language must be made aware of the similarities and differences of the two writing systems which are part of the two languages being studied.

73. BENJAMIN, Richard C. "A Bilingual Oral Language and Conceptual Development Program for Spanish-Speaking Pre-School Children," TESOL Quarterly. Volume 3, No. 4 (December 1969), pages 315-319. The TESOL Quarterly is an excellent journal for bilingual education teachers because the journal is concerned with teaching English to speakers of other languages.

74. BORREGO, Eva R. Teaching English As a Foreign Language to Children: First Three Grades. San Francisco: R&E Research Associates, 1974. For the primary school teacher who teaches non-English-speaking and non-English-dominant pupils. Soft cover.

75. BOWEN, Donald J. (editor). Techniques and Prodedures in Second Language Teaching. Quezon City: Alemar-Phoenix Publishing House, Inc. , no date. There are special instructional methods and techniques which a teacher must utilize when teaching English to students whose primary language is not English. Bowen's book elaborates on these special teaching procedures.

76. BRUCK, Margaret. "Language Impaired Children's Performance in an Additive Bilingual Education Program," Applied Psycholinguistics, Volume 3, No. 1 (March 1982), pages 45-60. The author discusses the positive effects which language impaired kindergarten and first grade children can obtain from being taught to read, write and do mathematics in a second language before they are taught these skills in their first language.

77. BURT, Marina, and Mary Finocchiaro (editors). Viewpoints on English as a Second Language. New York: Regents Publishing Company, 1977. A recommended text for the educator who wants to understand second language instructional methodology.

78. CARPENTER, Iris. "Babel Reversed, "American Education, Volume 13, No. 7 (August-September 1977), pages 27-30. This article describes the educational program at an elementary school where the 750 students come

from 50 different countries and collectively speak 27 different languages. The author mentions that the school uses an ESL instructional program to teach this linguistically diverse student population.

79. DACANAY, F. R. Techniques and Procedures in Second Language Teaching. Dobb's Ferry, New York: Oceans Publications, Inc. , 1963. An extremely useful text. English as a second language instructors, whether working for the federal government or for a public school district, will want Decanay's book in their personal library.

80. DENEMARK, G. W. "Why Teach Children a Foreign Language?" National Elementary Principal, Volume 39, No. 6 (1960), pages 6-11. What are the reasons for teaching students a second language? Denemark's article cogently answers this question. Recommended reading for opponents of bilingual education.

81. EBEL, Carolyn W. "Update: Teaching Reading to Students of English as a Second Language," The Reading Teacher, Volume 33, No. 4 (January 1980), pages 403-407. This article discusses the three historical trends in teaching ESL to students in the United States.

82. ENGLE, Patricia Lee. The Use of Vernacular Language in Education. Arlington, Virginia: The Center for Applied Linguistics, 1975. Children who cannot speak the national language can be taught it in one of two ways: (a) The Native Language Approach and (b) The Direct Method Approach. This work clearly explains how children can be taught a second language.

83. FINOCCHIARO, Mary. English as a Second Language: From Theory to Practice. New York: Simon and Schuster, 1964. The author is a nationally known expert on ESL (English as a second language) methodology. This is one of her better books on the subject. Recommended reading for students majoring in bilingual education.

84. _____. Teaching English as a Second Language. New York: Harper and Row, 1969. For the bilingual education major or bilingual education consultant who wants a broad understanding of ESL (English as a second language) instructional methodology. The author is an authority on ESL instruction.

85. _____, and Michael Bonomo. The Foreign Language Learner: A Guide for Teachers. New York: Regents Publishing Company, 1973. Teachers of students whose dominant language is not English will profit from the authors excellent book on second language learning. For ESL (English as a second language) instructors assigned to bilingual education components.

86. GILES, Howard, and Jane L. Byrne. "A Intergroup Approach to Second Language Acquisition," Journal of Multilingual and Multicultural Development, Volume 3, No. 1 (1982), pages 17-40. This lengthy article discusses the social and psychological factors which influence an individual's acquisition of a second language.

87. GONZALES, Phillip C. "Beginning English Reading for ESL Students," The Reading Teacher, Volume 35, No. 2 (November 1981), pages 154-161. The author discusses how to evaluate non-native English-speaking student's level of English competence and the structural level of reading material. Also discussed is when and how to introduce a non-native English speaker to initial reading instruction in English.

88. HABERMAN, Martin. "FLES: A Right Practice for the Wrong Reasons,"
National Elementary Principal, Volume 42 (May 1963), pages 51-54. The
author discusses the "right" reasons for teaching foreign languages in the
elementary school.

89. KOMACHIYA, Megumi. "Using a Wide Range of Activities to Foster Second Language Growth," Journal of Reading, Volume 25, No. 5 (February
1982), pages 436-438. A secondary school teacher of English as a second
language in Tokyo, Japan shares his most successful classroom experiences
and instructional activities with the reader.

90. KRASHEN, Stephen. Second Language Acquisition and Second Language
Learning. New York: Pergamon Press, 1981. This book makes available to teachers many important research findings on second language
acquisition.

91. LADO, Robert. Lado English Series. New York: Regents Publishing
Company, 1978. Adults who wish to learn English as a new language will
want to acquire the books in the Lado English series. Provided are basic
English language exercises for English language learners.

92. LAFAYETTE, Robert C. (editor). The Culture Revolution in Foreign Language Teaching. Skokie, Illinois: National Textbook Company, 1976.
This book of readings evaluates and explains the role of culture in foreign
or second language instruction.

93. LAMBERT, Wallace E., and G. R. Tucker. Bilingual Education of Children:
The St. Lambert Experiment. Rowley, Massachusetts: Newbury House
Publishers, Inc., 1972. Described is a bilingual study where Canadian
children at the kindergarten and elementary school level received their classroom
instruction in a foreign (second) language. The study presents evidence that
children can learn a new language more easily than many adults realize.

94. LIGHT, Richard L. "The Schools and the Minority Child's Language,"
1970. ERIC Microfiche, ED 047 320. A paper presented at the NCTE Convention, Atlanta, Georgia, November, 1970. Ten pages in length. Discussed are: (a) the history of bilingual education, (b) fear of diversity, and (c)
the child's first language.

95. LIN, San-su. Pattern Practice in the Teaching of Standard English to Students with a Non-Standard Dialect. New York: Teachers College Press,
1965. Students who speak a non-standard dialect of English should be
systematically exposed to the standard form of the English language. This is a
book for the teacher who wants to become more competent in language pattern
practice.

96. LUXENBERY, Stan. "Easing into English," American Education, Volume
17, No. 1 (January/February 1981), pages 31-36. The author explains
how the high schools in New York City are providing for the language needs
of non-English-speaking students.

97. MACNAMARA, John. "The Effects of Instruction in a Weaker Language,"
Journal of Special Issues, Volume 23, No. 2 (1967), pages 121-136. What
changes occur in individuals who receive instruction in their weaker language? Highly recommended reading for the graduate and undergraduate student
of bilingual education. Bilingual education consultants also will profit from reading this article.

98. MCDONOUGH, Steven H. *Psychology in Foreign Language Teaching.*
    Boston: George Allen & Unwin, 1981. Two chapters in this book are
    recommended reading for teachers in a bilingual classroom: (a) Chapter 7 -- "First Language Acquisition," and (b) Chapter 8 -- "Second Language Learning."

99. MICHIGAN MIGRANT PRIMARY INTER-DISCIPLINARY PROJECT. In-
    ter-disciplinary Oral Language Guide: Primary One, Part One: Lessons
    1-40. Michigan Oral Language Series. Standard English as a Second
    Language or Second Dialect. ACTF Edition, 1970. Contains numerous English
    oral language lessons which teachers can use in teaching English language
    structure to Spanish-dominant and Spanish-monolingual Mexican American
    students.

100. MIRANDA, Consuelo. "A Bilingual Oral Language and Conceptual Devel-
     opment Program for Spanish-Speaking Preschool Children," 1969. ERIC
     Microfiche, ED 034 568. Miranda's program is for Spanish-dominant
     children who need an English oral language foundation in order to succeed aca-
     demically in school.

101. MOLINA, Hubert. "Language Games and the Mexican-American Child
     Learning English," *TESOL* Quarterly, Volume 5 (June 1971), pages 145-
     148. Instructional games are useful in teaching English as a second
     (new) language to Spanish-dominant students. Molina's article is for teachers
     of Spanish-dominant Mexican American students and also for bilingual educa-
     tion majors.

102. PIERCE, J. *A Linguistic Method of Teaching a Second Language.* New
     York: Pageant, 1968. The author describes and discusses a unique
     method of teaching students a weaker language. For the bilingual edu-
     cation teacher assigned to an ESL (English as a second language) teaching as-
     signment who is searching for a linguistic approach to second language learn-
     ing.

103. POLITZER, Robert L., and Frieda N. Politzer. *Teaching English as a
     Second Language.* Lexington, Massachusetts: Xerox Publishing Com-
     pany, 1972. A well-written book for educational traditionalists who de-
     sire proficiency in ESL instructional methodology.

104. RAND, Elaine. "Elementary Second-Language Programs: How Bilingual
     Education Can Help," *Education Digest*, Volume 47, No. 8 (April 1982),
     pages 44-45. The author states that though bilingual education is not a
     foreign language program, it is geared to developing a student's proficiency
     in all aspects of two languages. Teachers trained in bilingual education also
     can be used to teach a second language to elementary school children.

105. RICHARDS, Jack C. (editor). *Understanding Second and Foreign Language
     Learning: Issues and Approaches.* Rowley, Massachusetts: Newbury
     House, 1978. This collection of papers should prove enlightening and
     useful to both the ESL teacher at the elementary school level and the EFL tea-
     cher at the college level. Length: 273 pages.

106. RITCHIE, William C. *Second Language Acquisition Research: Issues
     and Implications.* New York: Academic Press, 1978. Discussed are
     the various issues related to second language learning and teaching.

107. RIVERS, Wilga M. Teaching Foreign Language Skills. Chicago: The
       University of Chicago Press, 1965. Discussed are the language skills
       needed by second language learners. An outstanding text for the ESL
    instructor in a bilingual classroom.

108. SALINAS, Alicia M. "The Development of Communicative Competence
       in the Classroom," IDRA Newsletter, (September 1982), pages 6-8.
       Intercultural Development Research Association, 5835 Callaghan, San
    Antonio, Texas 78228. The author discusses some of the difficulties experi-
    enced by second language learners striving to achieve communicative compe-
    tence which are caused by the variety of language usage in the classroom.

109. SAMPSON, Gloria P. "Converging Evidence for a Dialectical Model of
       Function and Form in Second Language Learning," Applied Linguistics,
       Volume 3, No. 1 (Spring 1982), pages 1-28. Listed and discussed are
    thirteen facts about second language learning.

110. SEIDMAN, Dorles M. "Standard Oral English, Tenth Grade: Instructional
       Guide D." Los Angeles City Schools, California Division of Secondary
       Education, 1967. ERIC Microfiche, ED 027 352. The author states that
    oral language (speech) is the most common form of human communication.
    Yet, oral language frequently has received less emphasis in the classroom than
    have other means of communication. A publication full of educational data for
    high school teachers assigned to bilingual education programs.

111. SHEN, Yao. The Pronunciation of American English for Teachers of En-
       glish as a Foreign Language. Ann Arbor, Michigan: University of Mich-
       igan Press, 1964. Teachers of EFL (English as a Foreign Language)
    will find Shen's book an invaluable aid in helping foreign students master Amer-
    can English pronunciation.

112. SMITH, Marguerite. "English as a Second Language for Mexican Ameri-
       cans," no date. ERIC Microfiche, ED 016 560. For teachers who have
       Spanish-dominant Hispanic students in their classrooms but who are not
    familiar with ESL instructional strategies.

113. SORIANO, Jesse. "Spanish Guide, Kindergarten," Michigan Oral Language
       Series, 1970. ERIC Microfiche, ED 039 824. A guide for teaching Spanish
       oral language to kindergarten children.

114. SWAIN, Merrill. "Time and Timing in Bilingual Education," Language
       Learning, Volume 31, No. 1 (June 1981), pages 1-15. The author dis-
       cusses the effect that amount of time devoted to studying a second lan-
    guage has on second language proficiency. Also discussed is the importance
    of timing (when to introduce a language) in a bilingual classroom. This is an
    important article because it delves into the rationale of teaching two languages
    to children and the importance of timing in language introduction.

115. THONIS, Eleanor. Teaching Reading to Non-English Speakers. New York:
       Collier-MacMillan International, 1970. A quality book for the teacher of
       non-English-dominant students. This text should appeal to the professor
    of bilingual education.

116. WASSERMAN, Susan. "Raising the English Language Proficiency of Mexi-
       can American Children in the Primary Grades," California English Journal,
       Volume 6 (April 1970), pages 22-27. Elementary school teachers who

have disadvantaged Mexican American children in their classrooms will profit from reading Wasserman's method of increasing Mexican American pupils' English language competence.

117. WEST, Michael. Teaching English in Difficult Circumstances: Teaching English as a Foreign Language. London: Longmans Green, 1960. West's book is an excellent source for instructors who are assigned to the complicated challenge of teaching English to students who know few concepts in the English language.

118. YAWKEY, Thomas D. "Teaching Oral Language to Young Mexican- Americans," Elementary English, (February 1974), pages 198-202. Recommended for the teacher who is not skilled in second language teaching methodology.

III

BILINGUAL STUDENTS

A bilingual student is one who can communicate in two languages. Most educators agree that a student who can speak two languages has a linguistic advantage over a student who can speak only one language.

If bilingualism is considered to be a personal asset by most persons, why are so many bilingual students in the United States experiencing academic problems in the nation's public schools? In particular, why do so many bilingual Mexican American students underachieve in the classroom? Perhaps bilingualism is not the cause of bilingual students' academic underachievement. Perhaps such factors as low socioeconomic status, broken homes, ethnic isolation, inadequate educational programs, unqualified, undedicated and insensitive teachers, large class size, and lack of academic counseling are causing many bilingual students to experience academic difficulties in the classroom. It is lamentable that an asset such as childhood bilingualism should become a disadvantage simply because most American public schools are not prepared to teach bilingual children who are not English-dominant.

The selections below discuss the assets, academic problems and educational needs of America's bilingual students.

119. ANDERSSON, Theodore. "A New Focus on the Bilingual Child," The Modern Language Journal, Volume 49, No. 3 (March 1965), pages 156-160. The author emphasizes that in bilingual education programs, instruction should be done in Spanish and in English in such proportion as to increase the student's sense of security. Also discussed are bilingualism and the self-concept.

120. BLANCO, George. "Texas Report on Education for Bilingual Students," November 10, 1967. ERIC Microfiche, ED 017 388. The author discusses the instructional needs of non-English-speaking children in Texas.

121. CHRISTIAN, Chester C. "The Acculturation of the Bilingual Child," Modern Language Journal, Volume 49 (March 1965), pages 160-165. This article discusses how many bilingual children come to school psychologically and culturally prepared to function in a realm of thought different from that available to them in English. Recommended reading for teachers of Hispanic American children.

122. DIAZ, Joseph O. Prewitt. "Considerations for the development of a Reading Program for Puerto Rican Bilingual Students," Reading Improvement, Volume 18, No. 4 (Winter 1981), pages 302-307. The author discusses the role of reading in bilingual education. Some concepts mentioned are: (a) cognitive development theory, (b) English communication skills, (c) intensive English, (d) linguistically different children, (e) self-esteem, and (f) reading comprehension.

123. FANTINI, Alvino E. Language Acquisition of a Bilingual Child: A So-
     ciolinguistic Perspective. Brattleboro, Vermont: Experiment Press,
     1976. This text is for the teacher of bilingual students who wants ad-
ditional insights into the process whereby bilingual children acquire language
concepts in two languages.

124. FELDMAN, Carol, and Michael Shen. "Some Language-Related Cogni-
     tive Advantages of Bilingual 5-Year-Olds," 1969. ERIC Microfiche,
     ED 031 307. Are there intellectual and academic advantages in being
bilingual? The authors of this work cite the advantages of childhood bilingualism.

125. GALBRAITH, C. K. "Spanish-Speaking Children Communicate," Child-
     hood Education, Volume 42 (October 1965), pages 70-74. All normal
     children are able to communicate and bilingual Spanish-speaking child-
ren are no exception. Unfortunately, some monolingual English-speaking teachers erroneously conclude that because they and their Spanish-dominant students have difficulty communicating, Spanish-dominant students must be unable to communicate. Yet, these same children have no difficulty in being
understood within their community and at home. Highly recommended reading for teachers of Spanish-speaking elementary school students who believe
that some Spanish-speaking children cannot communicate.

126. GARCIA, E. E. "A Developmental Study of Spanish-English Production
     in Bilingual Children," Journal of Education Psychology. Volume 71
     (April 1979), pages 161-168. For the educator doing research on child-
hood bilingualism.

127. GONZALEZ, Gustavo. The Acquisition of Spanish Grammar by Native
     Spanish Speaking Children. Rosslyn, Virginia: National Clearinghouse
     for Bilingual Education, 1978. An important source for educators of
Hispanic children who want to learn about the type of Spanish vocabulary and
concepts acquired by Spanish-dominant students. This study shows that Spanish-dominant Mexican American students have a well-developed Spanish grammar which too often is not recognized and appreciated by non-Hispanic teachers.

128. GOODMAN, Lillian. "Juan's Right to Read," American Education, Vol-
     ume 6 (July 1970), pages 3-6. Some Hispanic students, because of their
     different linguistic background, have difficulty learning to read in the
English language. All students, whether bilingual or monolingual, have the
right to be taught by competent teachers who understand the unique learning
problems of Spanish-dominant students. Recommended reading for teachers
of Spanish-speaking students.

129. GUERRA, Emilio L. "Training Teachers for Spanish-Speaking Children
     on the Mainland," 1970. ERIC Microfiche, ED 046 300. Hispanic stu-
     dents in the United States belong to various cultural groups. Students of
Puerto Rican, Cuban, Mexican, Central American, and South American ancestry are examples of Hispanic student cultural groups which can be found in
our nation's classrooms. Teachers who have students from these cultural
groups in their classrooms need special training in order to cope with the
unique educational needs of many of these Hispanic students. Teachers of
Puerto Rican students will find that this publication discusses many educational
problems faced by teachers assigned to schools with a large Puerto Rican student enrollment.

130. HALL, Beverly. "Colorado's Lucky Children" The Bilingual, Bicult-
      ural Schools," The Nation, Volume 223 (November 20, 1976), pages 519-
      522. The author describes Colorado's bilingual-bicultural education
system which serves a public school student population which is 22 percent
Hispanic. Stressed is the fact that Colorado has both bilingual and bicultural
education.

131. JOHN, Vera P. , and Vivian M. Horner. "Bilingualism and the Spanish-
      speaking Child," in Chapter 8 of Language and Poverty by Frederick
      Williams. Chicago. Markham Publishing Company, 1970. Most language
authorities agree that the ability to communicate in two languages is a personal asset. Nevertheless, many Spanish-speaking students appear to be handicapped by their bilingualism. The authors discuss some of the language problems of many Spanish-speaking children.

132. KEITH, Mary T. "Sustained Primary Program for Bilingual Students,"
      1969. A paper presented at the International Reading Association Con-
      ference, Kansas City, Missouri, April 30-May 3, 1969. ERIC Micro-
fiche, ED 030 550. Bicultural curriculum, cultural values, self-concept, teacher aides, and non-graded education are discussed.

133. KNIEFEL, Tanya Suarez. "Programs Available for Strengthening the
      Education of Spanish-Speaking Students," Paper prepared for the Con-
      ference on Teacher Education for Mexican Americans, New Mexico
State University, February 13-15, 1969. ERIC Microfiche, ED 025 366. Discussed is Title VII of the Elementary and Secondary Education Act of 1965
which provides for the education of bilingual students.

134. KOO, John H. , and R. N. St. Clair (editors). Bilingual Education for
      Asian Americans: Problems and Strategies. Hiroshima, Japan: Bunka
      Hyoron Publishing Company, 1980. This book discusses the bilingual
education of Chinese American, Japanese American and Korean American
children. Length: 196 pages.

135. MANUEL, Herschel T. Spanish-Speaking Children of the Southwest --
      Their Education and the Public Welfare. Austin, Texas: University of
      Texas Press, 1965. The author discusses the various educational pro-
blems of Spanish-speaking students who reside in the Southwest. Also discussed are such topics as English as a second language, nongraded schools,
television, and dual language deficiencies.

136. MARCOUX, Fred W. Handicaps of Bilingual Mexican Children. San
      Francisco: R&E Research Associates, 1973. For the graduate student
      doing research on the disadvantaged Mexican American child. Soft
cover.

137. MARTINEZ, Armando. "Literacy Through Democratization of Educa-
      tion," Harvard Educational Review, Volume 40 (May 1970), pages 280-
      282. The author stresses that the chronic educational problems con-
fronting the Hispanic student can only be eliminated if educators become will-
ing to make provisions in the classroom for the cultural and linguistic rights
of all citizens. Recommended reading for future teachers and graduate students in bilingual education programs.

138. NEY, J. W. "Predator or Pedagogue?: The Teacher of the Bilingual
      Child," English Record, (April 1971), pages 12-18. The insensitive

teacher of Spanish-dominant students sometimes can do more harm than good in the classroom. Suggested reading for all teachers of bilingual students.

139. PIALORSI, Frank P. (editor). Teaching the Bilingual: New Methods and Old Traditions. Tucson, Arizona: University of Arizona Press, 1974.
A book suitable as a textbook in an undergraduate bilingual education methodology course.

140. QUINTANILLA, Guadalupe C. , and James B. Silman. Español: Lo Esencial Para el Bilingüe. Washington, D.C.: University Press of America, 1977. This volume is designed to aid in developing an ethnic identity for the Mexican American student. Explored are Mexican American cultural history, women's roles, religious customs and folklore. Recommended for the Spanish-dominant Mexican American university student who intends to become a bilingual education teacher.

141. RODRIGUEZ, Richard. "Aria: A Memoir of a Bilingual Childhood," The American Scholar, Volume 50, (Winter 1980/81), pages 25-42. The author explains the problems he faced as he grew up as a Mexican American from a Spanish-speaking home who learned English but forgot his Spanish as he progressed through school.

142. ROUCHDY, Aleya. Variation on a Theme: Bilingualism, A Case Study. Bloomington, Indiana: Indiana University Publications, 1977. The author discusses language tests administered to a bilingual child. The conclusions of this important study on bilingualism are presented in Chapter 5.

143. SIMOES, Antonio. The Bilingual Child: Research and Analysis of Existing Educational Themes. New York: Academic Press, 1976. One of the better books on America's bilingual student population which can be used as a supplementary text in some bilingual-bicultural education graduate courses.

144. SMITH, M. E. "A Study of the Speech of Eight Bilingual Children of the Same Family," Child Development, Volume 6, No. 1 (1935), pages 19-25. The author in this linguistic study, analyzed and compared the speech patterns of eight youthful bilingual family members. This study should appeal to linguists interested in childhood bilingualism.

145. SOUTHWEST COUNCIL OF FOREIGN LANGUAGE TEACHERS. "Our Bilingual -- Social and Psychological Barriers, Linguistic and Pedagogical Barriers," Second Annual Conference of the Southwest Council of Foreign Language Teachers, El Paso, Texas, November 13, 1965. ERIC Microfiche, ED 019 899. Some concepts discussed are; (a) remedial language instruction, (b) the Mexican American child, (c) school achievement, (d) mother tongue, (e) bilingual education, and (f) the educational needs of the bilingual child.

146. SPOERL, D. T. "The Academic and Verbal Adjustment of College-Age Bilingual Students," Journal of Genetic Psychology, Volume 64 (1974), pages 139-157. Many bilingual students who graduate from our nation's public schools decide to pursue a college degree. How well do bilingual students fare in college compared to monolingual students? Is bilingualism an asset or a handicap to college students? In this lengthy article, Spoerl describes the scholastic adjustment of bilingual college students and discusses many of the factors which are associated with the academic success and failure of college-age bilingual students.

147. UNITED STATES BUREAU OF INDIAN AFFAIRS. Bilingual Education
     for American Indians. New York: Arno Press, 1978. The book dis-
     cusses the many educational problems of American Indian children and
how a bilingual education can help make schooling a meaningful and rewarding
experience for most American Indian children.

148. ZOBEL, Jan. "The Mexican-American School Child," Illinois Schools
     Journal, (Summer 1970), pages 103-113. How does the Mexican Amer-
     ican public school student differ from other public school students? Do
Mexican American students have unique educational needs? These and other
questions are answered in this provocative publication.

IV

TEACHER EDUCATION
AND STAFF DEVELOPMENT

It is a safe conjecture that the majority of teachers assigned to teach Spanish-dominant Hispanic American students are not adequately prepared to teach this group of learners. Few teachers have received training in such areas as Spanish reading methodology, language assessment, English as a second language, Spanish as a second language, oral language development, individualized instruction, parent involvement, teacher aide utilization, and bilingual curriculum development. The days are gone when an English mono-lingual teacher could expect to continue using ineffective instructional methods to teach non-English-speaking and non-English-dominant students. Today, an unqualified teacher is expected to master those instructional skills which will qualify him or her to meet the unique educational needs of his students.

Most universities that have teacher education programs are not pre-paring future teachers who will be competent to teach linguistically different and culturally different children. Fortunately, each year more American universities are offering bilingual-bicultural education programs and multi-cultural education programs to their education majors. Also, many school districts that serve Hispanic children are successfully reeducating their edu-cators by providing them with a staff development program that will prepare educators for linguistically and culturally different children.

149. ACOSTA, Robert, and George Blanco. Competencies for University Programs in Bilingual Education. Washington, D. C. : Superintend-ent of Documents, U.S. Government Printing Office, 1978. This book-let is a concise introduction to competencies appropriate for undergraduate, master's level and doctoral teacher training programs in bilingual education.

150. BALLESTEROS, Octavio A. Preparing Teachers for Bilingual Educa-tion: Basic Readings. Washington, D. C.: University Press of Amer-ica, 1979. The articles in this collection cover such topics as: (a) linguistics, (b) sociology, (c) psychology, (d) the Spanish language, (e) the Mexican culture, and (f) bilingual teaching methodology. Length: 215 pages. Soft cover.

151. BATY, R. M. Reeducating Teachers for Cultural Awareness Prepara-tion for Educating Mexican-American Children in California. New York: Praeger Publishers, 1972. This book presents the results of an educa-tional study to determine the effects of teacher inservice training on selected attitudes of elementary school teachers. Recommendations concerning inser-vice training are presented.

152. BORDIE, John. "Cultural Sensitivity Training for the Teacher of Span-ish-Speaking Children, " TESOL Quarterly, Volume 4 (December 1970),

pages 337-342. A provocative article for bilingual education program teachers which explains the need to make educators more sensitive to the cultural and linguistic needs of their Hispanic students.

153. CARRILLO, Federico M. The Development of a Rationale and Model
     Program to Prepare Teachers for the Bilingual-Bicultural Secondary
     School Programs. San Francisco: R&E Research Associates, 1977.
For secondary school educators whose schools have a predominantly Mexican American student enrollment. Soft cover.

154. CEJA, Manuel V. Methods of Orientation of Spanish-Speaking Child-
     ren to an American School. San Francisco: R&E Research Associates,
     1973. For education teachers who want to make school enrollment a
pleasant experience for Hispanic children. Soft cover.

155. CHALL, Jeanne. Learning to Read: The Great Debate. New York:
     McGraw-Hill Book Company, Inc. , 1968. A "must" book for the bi-
     lingual elementary school teacher who is baffled by the poor reading
skills of so many elementary school students.

156. FILLMORE, Lily Wong. "Language Minority Students and School Par-
     ticipation: What Kind of English is Needed?" Journal of Education,
     Volume 164, No. 2 (Spring 1982), pages 143-156. The author contends
that one of the most complex and serious problems for American schools is
the education of students whose primary language is not English. The main
challenge of educators is to determine what language skills students need in
order to successfully function in school. It is important that non-English-
speaking students and limited-English-speaking students be provided with bilingual instruction until they can function in English.

157. GARFINKEL, Alan, and Stanley Hamilton (editors). Designs for Foreign
     Language Teacher Education. Rowley, Massachusetts: Newbury House
     Publishers, Inc. , 1976. This text can be used to prepare teachers for
non-English home language learners.

158. GILES, Mary B., and T. M. Sherman. "Measurement of Multicultural
     Attitudes of Teacher Trainees," The Journal of Educational Research,
     Volume 75, No. 4 (March/April 1982); pages 204-209. The authors
discuss the Multicultural Attitude Questionnaire (MAQ), an instrument which
can be used to assess multicultural attitudes of future teachers and practicing
teachers.

159. JOHNSON, Kenneth R. "Teaching Culturally Disadvantaged Pupils,"
     1967. ERIC Microfiche, ED 029 930. The author stresses that for
     culturally disadvantaged children, the lack of opportunity to come into
contact with the language system of the middle class culture is educationally
penalizing. The author contends that standard English should be taught as an
alternate dialect to speakers of nonstandard dialects.

160. LATIMER, Betty. "Telegraphing Messages to Children About Minori-
     ties," Reading Teacher, (November 1976), pages 152-156. An impor-
     tant article for teachers of minority group students which explains how
we convey our attitudes toward minorities to our children.

161. LÓPEZ, Thomas F. "Staff Development of Bilingual Programs," Un-
     published Master's Thesis, Sacramento State College, 1970. ERIC Mi-
     crofiche, ED 044 233. Discussed are: the self-concept, history of

bilingual education, cultural values, and staff development. In this study, the author contends that if the public schools rejects the mother tongue of an entire group of children such as the Spanish spoken by Hispanic students, this language rejection can be expected to adversely affect these students' concept of self, home, and their ethnic group. A definition of bilingual education is provided.

162. MOSES LAKE INTERMEDIATE SCHOOL DISTRICT 104, STATE OF WASHINGTON. "Mexican American Cultural Differences: A Brief Survey to Enhance Teacher-Pupil Understanding," Office of Education (DHEW), Washington, D.C., 1969. ERIC Microfiche, ED 041 665. This publication is recommended reading for future teachers and practicing teachers who anticipate teaching in an elementary school with a large Mexican American student enrollment.

163. PACHECO, Manuel T. "Preparing Teachers for Non-English Home Language Learners," in Alan Garfinkel (editor). Design for Foreign Language Teacher Education. Rowley, Massachusetts: Newbury House Publishers, 1976. This article is for the elementary school teacher who has Spanish-dominant children in his or her classroom who needs to find effective ways to instruct this group of children.

164. PALOMARES, U. H. "Communication Begins with Attitude," National Elementary Principal, Volume 50 (November 1970), pages 47-49. The instructional effectiveness or lack of instructional effectiveness of teachers is definitely affected by the teachers' positive or negative attitudes toward the students they teach. An informative article on teacher attitudes.

165. "Preparing for Bilingual Education," no author. American Education, Volume 13, No. 7 (August-September 1977), pages 31-32. A short article which lists the American states which have federally funded university bilingual education training and fellowship awards and the languages in which future bilingual education teachers are being trained.

166. RODRÍGUEZ, Louis P. "Preparing Teachers for the Spanish Speaking," National Elementary Principal, Volume 50 (November 1970), pages 50-52. An article which contains specific suggestions for preparing teachers who lack the instructional competency to teach non-English-dominant Spanish-speaking students.

167. SUTMAN, Francis X. Educating Personnel for Bilingual Settings: Present and Future. Washington, D.C.: American Association of Colleges for Teacher Education, 1979. Discussed are: (a) current trends in bilingual teacher training, (b) guidelines for program design and development in teacher education, and (c) criteria for evaluating teaching performance.

168. TEEL, D. "Preventing Prejudice Against Spanish-Speaking Children," Educational Leadership, Volume 12 (November 1954), pages 94-98. Ways of preventing and reducing hostile attitudes toward Hispanic students are discussed. Recommended reading for bilingual education program teachers who wish to better understand the causes of ethnic prejudice. An old but valid article.

169. TEXAS EDUCATION AGENCY. Bilingual Education K-3 Resource Manual. Austin, Texas: Division of Bilingual Education, TEA, 1977. A resource guide for teachers of Spanish-speaking bilingual students in grades kindergarten through third.

170. TIREMAN, Lloyd. Teaching Spanish-speaking Children. New York:
Arno Press, 1976. A book which can be used as a supplementary text
in an undergraduate bilingual-bicultural education methodology course.

171. WALSH, Sister Marie Andre. The Development of a Rationale for a
Program to Prepare Teachers for Spanish-Speaking Children in the Bilingual-bicultural Elementary School. San Francisco: R&E Research
Associates, 1976. A technical publication for the educator searching for a
philosophy of bilingual and bicultural education. Soft cover.

172. WEBER, Christian O. Basic Philosophies of Education. New York:
Holt, Rinehart, and Winston, 1960. Though bilingual education is not
discussed in this work, Weber's text provides the reader with a broad
view of the "classic" educational philosophies prevalent today in American
education. Some of the philosophies outlined are: (a) idealism, (b) realism,
(c) pragmatism, (d) essentialism, and (e) traditionalism. For the educator
who needs to develop a sound philosophy of education. Hard cover.

173. ZINTZ, Miles. "What Classroom Teachers Should Know About Bilingual
Education," College of Education, University of New Mexico, Albuquerque, New Mexico, 1969. ERIC Microfiche, ED 028 427. The author
makes the important point that language is personal and that language reflects
the individual's self-image and is his or her only avenue to expressing all
that he or she is, all that he or she has as a heritage, and all that he or she
aspires to become. Recommended reading for bilingual education consultants
and school administrators.

V

PROGRAMS, CURRICULUM,
INSTRUCTION, AND MATERIALS

Bilingual education is the use of two languages in the classroom as mediums of instruction. It is difficult to conceive that a bilingual education program can exist without a concomitant bicultural education program.

Bicultural education is an education program where students learn about the history, culture and social contributions of their home culture and the national culture.

Schools that serve linguistically and culturally different children need to develop and utilize programs, curricula, instructional methods, and instructional materials which will serve the educational needs of these children.

Much has been said about the dire need for bilingual curricula and materials in schools with bilingual education programs. Nevertheless, few educators, writers, and publishers seem to be involved in the production of books and materials for this neglected but important field.

The sources in this section cover such topics as (a) curricular materials for bilingual-bicultural education, (b) the teaching of reading in a pluralistic classroom, (c) teaching in a multicultural classroom, (d) multiethnic readers, (e) bilingual materials development, (f) reading programs and reading exercises for Mexican American children, (g) the curricular needs of Mexican American children, (h) bilingual-bicultural programs for preschool children, (i) instructional priorities in a culturally pluralistic school, (j) Hispanic folklore, (k) Hispanic dances, stories and poetry, and (l) bilingual instructional methodology.

174. ADKINS, Patricia G. "Speech for the Spanish-Speaking Student," The Bulletin of the National Association of Secondary School Principals, No. 350 (December 1970), pages 108-113. The author mentions such topics as oral communication, valuing a child's native language, teacher expectations, teacher attitudes, and cultural heritage.

175. _____. "Teaching Idioms and Figures of Speech to Non-Native Speakers of English," Modern Language Journal, Volume 52 (March 1968), pages 148-152. Suggested reading for teachers in bilingual education programs who need more information in the area of language instruction methodology.

176. AGUIRRE, Rueben E. Teaching the Chicano/Mexican American Cultural Heritage in the Elementary School: A Teacher's Guide Part I and Part II. San Francisco: R&E Research Associates, 1977. A technical text for the scholar doing educational research on ways to include the Mexican American cultural legacy into the curriculum of the elementary grades. Soft cover.

177. ALMARAZ, Felix D. Reading Exercises on Mexican Americans. Elizabethtown, Pennsylvania: The Continental Press, 1977. This soft cover

publication was designed for Mexican American students in the Southwest. Basically the book is a series of short stories about famous Mexican
Americans and their accomplishments. At the end of each story are questions
to be answered by the student.

178. AMSDEN, Constance. "A Reading Program for Mexican American
       Children," 1965. ERIC Microfiche, ED 016 757. Most middle class
       teachers are not aware that disadvantaged Spanish-dominant students
often require a special type of reading program. Amsden's publication describes a reading program for Mexican American students which shows pro-
mise.

179. ANGEL, Frank. "Program Content to Meet the Educational Needs of
       Mexican-Americans," 1968. ERIC Microfiche, ED 017 392. Discussed
       are: (a) the special educational needs of Mexican American students,
(b) the need for curricular change, (c) oral language programs, (d) the effective
domain, and (e) career education.

180. ARENAS, Soledad. "Bilingual/Bicultural Programs for Preschool
       Children," Children Today, (July/August 1978). This article should be
       of interest to teacher aides serving in a preschool classroom who plan
to become teachers.

181. ARNOLD, Richard D. "Components of a Reading Program for the Mex-
       ican-American Child," Paper presented at the International Reading
       Association Conference, Anaheim, California, May 6-9, 1970. ERIC
Microfiche, 040 026. The author discusses the nine criteria applicable to
reading programs for Mexican American children. Also discussed are: (a)
reading problems, (b) remedial reading programs, (c) teacher aides, (d) instructional services, and (e) reading as a pleasant experience.

182. BAKER, Gwendolyn C. "Instructional Priorities in a Culturally Plural-
       istic School," Educational Leadership, Volume 32 (December 1974),
       pages 176-178. How does teaching in a multicultural school differ from
teaching in a monocultural school? This and other questions about multicultural education are discussed in Baker's article.

183. BALLESTEROS, José Ramón. Origen y Evolución Del Charro Mexicano.
       Santa Monica, California: Libros Latinos, 1972. A charro is a Mexican
       cowboy. Mexicans love their charros in much the same way that Ameri-
cans love their cowboys. Ballesteros provides the reader with a history of
the Mexican cowboy. This work can be used as a social studies reference book
by Spanish monolingual high school students enrolled in a bilingual-bicultural
education program. Written in Spanish.

184. BALLESTEROS, Octavio A. Mexican Proverbs: The Philosophy, Wis-
       dom and Humor of a People. Burnet, Texas: Eakin Publications, 1979.
       A collection of 367 Mexican proverbs translated into English from the
Spanish. This bilingual book can be used as a supplementary Spanish textbook
or as a library book in schools with an English-Spanish bilingual education
program. Hard cover.

185. BARLOW, Genevieve. Leyendas Mexicanas: A Collection of Mexican
       Legends. Skokie, Illinois: National Textbook Company, 1979. Each
       legend is followed by exercises. This book can be used as a supplement-
ary cultural reader in the English-Spanish bilingual classroom. A Spanish
language book.

186. BEALS, Carleton. Stories Told by the Aztecs Before the Spanish Came. New York: Abelard-Schuman, 1970. This charming book contains many pre-Spanish legends which are an important part of Mexico's Aztec heritage. Recommended for Mexican American teenagers enrolled in an American English-Spanish bilingual-bicultural education program.

187. BROOKS, B. David. "Strategies for Teaching Within a Bicultural Setting," Reading Improvement, Volume 13 (Summer 1976), pages 86-91. A valuable source for teachers of bicultural students. Recommended reading for English monolingual teachers in bilingual education.

188. BURKE, Loretta. Let's Play Games in Spanish Volume One. Skokie, Illinois: National Textbook Company, 1968. For Spanish teachers in elementary and secondary school who realize that educational games are an effective method of teaching students a first or second language.

189. CARTER, Robert F. Mexico: Historia Simplificada/ A Simplified History. New York: Regents Publishing Company, 1977. For the casual reader who wants an umcomplex narrative of the history of Mexico. A bilingual book which can serve as a reference book in a secondary English-Spanish bilingual-bicultural education program.

190. CHASE, Josephine, and Linda Parth. Multicultural Spoken Here. Santa Monica, California: Goodyear Publishing Company, 1979. Ideas and activities for teaching multicultural awareness in grades three through six. Length: 120 pages.

191. CHEYNEY, Arnold B. "Teaching Children of Different Cultures in the Classroom: A Language Approach," 1976. ERIC Microfiche, ED 120 811. Also published in book form by Charles E. Merrill Publishing Company. Teachers who find themselves assigned to teach in a multicultural classroom often realize that their college education has not prepared them for such an assignment. This publication addresses itself to this multifaceted educational issue.

192. DE CASARE, Ruth. Canciones para la clase de español. Belivin Publishing Corporation. Melville, New York 11746, 1969. Teachers of Spanish will want to teach the songs in this interesting book to their students. Songs for various occasions.

193. DEDERA, Don, and Bob Robles. Goodbye, Garcia, Adios. Flagstaff, Arizona: Northland Press, 1978. Written in a bilingual format. Appropriate for high school students in an English-Spanish bilingual education program.

194. DIXON, Robert J., and Herbert Fox. Mi Primer Diccionario Illustrado de Ingles. New York: Regents Publishing Company, 1960. A beginner's illustrated English-Spanish language dictionary.

195. DOMÍNGUEZ, Sylvia M. La Comadre María. Austin: American Universal Artforms Corporation, 1973. A Spanish language comedy about Mexican Americans which can be used as a language arts book in a secondary bilingual-bicultural education program. Seventy-five pages in length.

196. DURHAM, Joseph T. "Who Needs It? Compensatory Education," The

<u>Clearinghouse</u>, Volume 44 (September 1969), pages 18-22. The author discusses eight characteristics of compensatory education programs for Mexican American pupils.

197. EPSTEIN, Sam. <u>The First Book of Mexico</u>. New York: Franklin Watts, Inc., 1967. A book suitable for secondary school libraries that serve an English-Spanish bilingual-bicultural education program and for individuals and organizations forming a "Mexico" collection.

198. FLORES, Angel (editor). <u>Spanish Stories/Cuentos Españoles: A Bantam Dual-Language Book</u>. New York: Bantam Books, 1971. An excellent selection of Spanish language short stories translated into English which can be used by Spanish monolingual high school students who were born in Latin America. Paperback.

199. FOERSTER, Leona. "Teaching Reading in Our Pluralistic Classrooms," Reading Teacher, (November 1976), pages 146-150. A pluralistic classroom is one that contains students from various cultures and linguistic backgrounds. The teaching of reading in a pluralistic setting is a challenge for the average monolingual teacher. This article will shed light on ways to teach in a multicultural classroom.

200. FRANK, Virginia. "New Curricular Materials and the Teaching of the Disadvantaged," 1968. ERIC Microfiche, ED 027 246. School and home values, teacher developed materials, a relevant curriculum, cultural differences, and tutors are some of the topics mentioned in this work.

201. GARBER, Malcolm. "Classroom Strategies: Culture and Learning Styles," Southwest Cooperative Educational Laboratory, Albuquerque, New Mexico, 1968. ERIC Microfiche, ED 025 364. A child's cultural group membership has an effect on his learning style; a child's socioeconomic level also has an effect on his learning style and academic motivation. Garber's publication discusses instructional approaches which teachers of culturally different children can employ in the classroom.

202. GIRARD, Alexander. <u>The Magic of a People</u>. New York: The Viking Press, 1968. This is a Spanish-English bilingual book sixty-eight pages in length. Most of the book consists of colorful photographs of folk art and toys created by Latin American craftsmen. Soft cover.

203. GONZALEZ, Phillip. "English as a Second Language in Math Education," NABE Journal. Volume 5, No. 1 (Fall 1980), pages 93-101. The author describes a bilingual-bicultural elementary school program where children are given the opportunity to begin learning in their home language while gradually developing English language skills.

204. GRUBB, Susan A. " 'Back of the Yards' Goes Bilingual," <u>American Education</u>, Volume 12, (March 1976), pages 15-18. The author describes a bilingual-bicultural elementary school program where children are given the opportunity to begin learning in their home language while gradually developing English language skills.

205. HOLMAN, Rosemary. <u>Spanish Nuggets.</u> San Antonio: The Naylor Company, 1968. The reader who enjoys insights found in Mexican proverbs will enjoy the almost fifty Mexican proverbs in this hard cover volume. Each proverb is in Spanish and English. The book can be used in an elementary school with an English-Spanish bilingual education program.

206. HUCK, Charlotte S. "The Changing Character of Basic Reading Materials," Educational Leadership, Volume 22 (March 1965), pages 377-381.
Discussed are: (a) basic readers for the primary grades, (b) basic readers for the middle grades, (c) multi-ethnic readers, and (d) centralized school libraries. Suggested reading for the teacher in a multicultural classroom.

207. IBARRA, Herbert. "Teaching in Spanish to the Spanish Speaking," Foreign Language Annals, Volume 2, (March 1969), pages 310-315.
Spanish teachers are aware that English monolinguals should be taught Spanish by one method and that Spanish-English bilinguals should be taught Spanish by another method. Spanish teachers who have not mastered the two methods of teaching Spanish to their students should carefully read Ibarra's article.

208. JOHNSON, Edith. Regional Dances of Mexico. Chicago: Banks Upshaw and Company, 1963. Also published in 1974 by National Textbook Company, Skokie, Illinois. Bilingual education teachers will want to teach Mexican dances to their Mexican American pupils and this valuable book will aid them to accomplish this educational objective.

209. KAUFMAN, M. "Will Instruction in Reading Spanish Affect Ability in Reading English?" Journal of Reading, Volume 2 (April 1968), pages 521-527. Many bilingual education experts agree that teaching Spanish-dominant children to read initially in Spanish will have a positive effect on the children's ability to read in English. Kaufman's article explores the implications of providing children with dual language reading instruction.

210. LAREW, Leonor A. "English-Speaking Students Predominate in Bilingual Multicultural Program in Buffalo," Hispania, Volume 65, No. 1 (March 1982), pages 98-99. The author describes a bilingual-multicultural program in an elementary school in Buffalo, New York where only 124 of the school's 555 students were Spanish-speaking. The author explains why most of the students in this program were non-Hispanic English speakers.

211. LÓPEZ, Arcadia. Los animales del parque. Austin, Texas: American Universal Artforms Corporation, 1973. This booklet contains Spanish language animal vocabulary and can be used as a supplementary reader in the English-Spanish bilingual elementary school classroom. In Spanish only. Length: twenty-eight pages.

212. MACKEY, W. F. "A Typology of Bilingual Education," Foreign Language Annals, Volume 3, No. 4 (1970), pages 596-608. The author is an international authority on bilingual education. This scholarly article is highly recommended reading for all students of bilingual education. Various types of bilingual programs are mentioned.

213. MARTÍNEZ, Al. Rising Voices. New York: The New American Library, Inc., 1974. This work contains 52 brief biographies of outstanding Spanish-speaking Americans and can be used as a social studies reference book in an English-Spanish bicultural high school classroom. This text is available in Spanish. Photographs. Soft cover.

214. MILLER, Robert. "The Mexican Approach to Developing Bilingual Materials and Teaching Literacy to Bilingual Students," The Reading Teacher, Volume 35, No. 7 (April 1982), pages 800-804. Miller

describes how educators in Mexico develop and use bilingual materials in teaching reading to pupils in both their native language and the new language they are learning. Some American educators already are studying Mexico's method of teaching literacy in two languages to her linguistic minorities.

215. NEWLON, Clarke. Famous Mexican Americans. New York: Dodd, Mead and Company, 1972. Spanish-speaking high school students will be inspired by the lives of the prominant Mexican Americans mentioned in Newlon's quality book which can be used as a bicultural social studies reference book.

216. NOREEN, Sister, Daughter of Charity. "A Bilingual Curriculum for Spanish-Americans," Catholic School Journal, Volume 66 (January 1966), page 25. In this short but enlightening article on bilingual education for Mexican American students, the author points out that for too many years, Spanish-dominant students have been erroneously classified as mentally retarded when in reality they have been only bilingually deficient. A valuable article for future teachers who anticipate teaching in the Southwest.

217. PAZ, Octavio (editor). An Anthology of Mexican Poetry. Bloomington: Indiana University Press, 1969. A collection of sensitive poetry collected by Paz, who has an international reputation as a poet. Paz was born in Mexico. This anthology can be used in the English-Spanish high school bilingual classroom as a language arts poetry book.

218. PERALES, A. M. "The Audio-Lingual Approach and the Spanish Student," Hispania, Volume 48 (March 1965), pages 98-102. Discussed are such topics as: (a) the Mexican American student's language problem, (b) materials and methods for teaching Spanish-dominant students, (c) language development, and (d) oral language experiences.

219. PEREZ, Samuel A. "How to Effectively Teach Spanish-Speaking Children Even if You're Not Bilingual," Language Arts, Volume 54 (February 1979), pages 159-162. The author gives various instructional suggestions to monolingual teachers of Spanish-speaking students. Some examples of instructional suggestions are: (a) team teaching, (b) bilingual teacher aides, (c) peer teaching, and (d) parental involvement.

220. PETTIT, Florence H. Mexican Folk Toys. New York: Hastings House, 1979. Mexican artisans produce hundreds of handmade toys which for decades have been the delight of Mexico's children. These toys can be used by bilingual education program educators to decorate their classrooms. An attractively illustrated book.

221. PLATA, Maximino, and Priscilla Jones. "Bilingual Vocational Education for Handicapped Students," Exceptional Children, Volume 48, No. 6 (April 1982), pages 538-540. The authors discuss the roles of the good bilingual teacher and the special education teacher in a bilingual vocational education program for limited or non-English-speaking handicapped students.

222. RAMSEY, Patricia G. "Multicultural Education in Early Childhood," Young Children, Volume 37, No. 2 (January 1982), pages 13-23. The author stresses that all children in the United States need to understand the culturally pluralistic nature of American society and that multicultural education can be incorporated effectively into every aspect of an early childhood program.

223. RIVERA, Feliciano. "Curriculum and Materials for Bilingual, Bicult-
     ural Education," National Elementary Principal, Volume 50 (November
     1970), pages 56-61. Rivera provides some solutions to the curriculum
problems of bilingual-bicultural education programs for Spanish-speaking
students.

224. ROBINETT, Ralph. "Developing Curriculum for Bilingual Education,"
     1972. ERIC Microfiche, ED 061 811. Paper presented at the confer-
     ence on Child Development, Chicago, Illinois, November 22-24, 1972.
The author discusses the lack of curriculum materials for bilingual education
programs. Robinett mentions that neither curriculum components of bilingual
projects nor commercial interests have been able to keep pace in bilingual
curriculum development.

225. ROSEN, Carl L., and Philip D. Ortega. "Problems and Strategies
     in Teaching the Language Arts to Spanish Speaking Students," no date.
     ERIC Microfiche, ED 025 368. The authors discuss some of the in-
structional methods which can be utilized by educators when teaching language
arts to Hispanic students.

226. _____, and _____. "Programs Available for Strengthening the Edu-
     cation of Spanish Speaking Students," no date. ERIC Microfiche, ED
     025 366. The authors discuss some of the many educational programs
available to Spanish-dominant Hispanic students.

227. SAUVAGEAU, Juan. Stories That Must Not Die. Volumes I, II, and
     III. Austin, Texas: The Oasis Press, 1976. P.O. Box 1825, Austin,
     Texas 78767. Each volume contains ten folkloric stories about Mexi-
cans and Mexican Americans. At the end of each story are questions, vocabulary, and cognates. Each story is in English and Spanish.

228. SCHNEIDER, Velia. "Bilingual Lessons for Spanish-Speaking Pre-
     school Children," 1969. ERIC Microfiche, ED 031 465. Head Start
     teachers and kindergarten teachers who teach Spanish-dominant child-
ren will want to refer to the bilingual lessons in this publication.

229. SEPULVEDA, Betty R. "Teaching the Educationally Disadvantaged
     Hispano Child at the K-3 Level," 1970. ERIC Microfiche, ED 036 807.
     The author discusses a Formal Language Learning Program for educa-
tionally disadvantaged Spanish-speaking children. Ten objectives of the program are listed in this instructive publication.

230. SOFFIETTI, James P. "Why Children Fail to Read: A Linguistic Ana-
     lysis," Harvard Educational Review, Volume 25 (Spring 1955), pages
     63-84. A lengthy explanation of the many reasons why school children
fail to master the reading process. A linguistically oriented article for
reading specialists, reading researchers, and classroom teachers.

231. STOUT, Irving W., and Grace Langdon. "The Use of Toys in Teaching
     English to Non-English Speaking Children," College of Education, Ari-
     zona State University, 1964. ERIC Microfiche, ED 001 756. This ed-
ucational study was conducted to determine the effectiveness of educational
toys in teaching Spanish-dominant students in Arizona.

232. SUMPTER, Magdalena Benavides. Discovering Folklore Through Commu-
     nity Resources. Austin, Texas: Dissemination and Assessment Center
     for Bilingual Education, 1978. This book is concerned with the following

aspects of the Mexican American culture: (a) riddles, (b) customs and traditions, (c) proverbs, (d) tales, (e) herbs, and (f) faith healers. Hard cover.

233. TRESSELT, Alvin. El Viejo y el Tigre. New York: Grosset and Dun-
      lap, 1971. Most Spanish-speaking pupils enjoy having their teachers
      read them Spanish language tales. Tresselt's tale about an old man
and a tiger has already become a favorite with many Hispanic pupils.

234. TUCKER, G. R. "Some Thoughts Concerning Bilingual Education Pro-
      grams," The Modern Language Journal, Volume 55, No. 8 (1971),
      pages 491-493. Is bilingual education the panacea for the education-
al ills of disadvantaged Spanish-speaking students that many educators claim
it to be? In this publication, Tucker gives his thoughts on the effectiveness
of bilingual education programs in the United States.

235. UNITED STATES DEPARTMENT OF TRANSPORTATION. A Trip to
      the Airport/Un Viaje al Aeropuerto. Washington, D.C.: Federal
      Aviation Administration, U.S. Department of Transportation, no date.
This paperback booklet can be used by high school teachers who need bilingual materials for their Spanish-dominant students.

236. VELA, Irma Saldivar. Bailes a Colores. Austin, Texas: American
      Universal Artforms Corporation, 1972. A color-keyed system for
teaching popular Mexican dances. Length: seventy-one pages.

237. VERGARA, Lautaro. Dos Caminos. Quanah, Texas: Nortex Press,
      1977. A collection of bilingual poems that high school students in
English-Spanish bilingual education programs will enjoy reading.

238. VERNER, Zenobia, and Josue Gonzalez. "English Language Teaching
      in a Texas Bilingual Programme," English Language Teaching, Volume
      25, No. 3 (June 1971), pages 296-302. Some concepts discussed are:
(a) oral English, (b) non-English-speaking Mexican American first graders,
(c) unsuccessful reading achievement, (d) lack of English language experience, and (e) instructional materials.

239. WAHL, Jan. Cristobol and the Witch. New York: G. P. Putman's Sons,
      1972. This is the story of a young boy who meets a witch. A story
      specially written to appeal to Hispanic students which can be used as a
classroom library book in an English-Spanish bilingual classroom.

240. WAY, R. V. Adapting the Curriculum of an Elementary School to
      Serve the Language Needs of Spanish-Speaking Children. San Francisco:
      R&E Research Associates, 1974. As a school's student population
changes, so must the school's curriculum change. Too many educators
tend to violate this basic educational principle. The author of this technical
publication discusses the need to adapt a school's curriculum to meet the
linguistic needs of bilingual students. Soft cover.

241. WILLES, Burlington. Games and Ideas for Teaching Spanish. Belmont:
      Fearon Publishers, 1967. The effective Spanish teacher frequently
      will incorporate new instructional methods into his or her daily lesson
plans. Willes' book contains numerous ideas on ways that teachers can make
the teaching of Spanish more interesting to their students.

242. "The Windsor Hill School in Los Angeles," no author, Phi Delta Kappan,

Volume 51 (January 1970), page 292. The results reported in this
brief article could be inferred to the bilingual student. Described is
a school program where minority students are achieving academically at a
level comparable to middle class Anglo American students.

243. WOOD, Frances E. Enchantment of America, Mexico. Chicago:
      Childrens Press, 1964. A book for public school libraries with a
      large Spanish-speaking student enrollment. Wood's work leaves the
reader with a positive attitude toward our neighbor south of the Rio Grande.

244. YLISELA, James. "Language and Learning in Chicago," American
      Education, Volume 18, No. 4 (May 1982), pages 12-15. The author
      describes how the Chicago public schools turned six of its elementary
schools into language academies where students could study such foreign
languages as French, German, Modern Greek, Italian, Japanese, Polish,
Russian and Spanish. One of the six academies also offers an English-
Spanish bilingual education program.

245. YOES, Deck. "Reading Programs for Mexican-American Children of
      Texas," Reading Teacher, Volume 20 (January 1967), pages 313-318.
      The author describes reading programs which were instituted for Mex-
ican American students in three Texas cities -- El Paso, Del Rio, and Cor-
pus Christi. English-Spanish reading teachers will benefit from reading
Yoes' article.

246. YORIO, Carlos Alfredo. "Extra-Curricular Mini-Courses as Part of
      the Curriculum of a Course in English as a Foreign Language," 1973.
      ERIC Microfiche, ED 082 586. One way of teaching EFL (English as
a Foreign Language) to students is to offer extra-curricular mini-courses.
In this way, the student who is weak in English will be provided with additional opportunities to strengthen his English language concepts. Teachers
of non-English-dominant students will find value in Yorio's publication.

VI

LANGUAGE AND LINGUISTICS

Language may be defined as a culture's system of vocal symbols which allows a person who has mastered it to communicate with another person who has mastered the same system. Language also may be defined as the vehicle of culture.

It is important for teachers to understand how children acquire language. Teachers assigned to a bilingual classroom should be familiar with ways of developing English language proficiency in students whose dominant language is not English.

Many Hispanic American students who enroll in American public schools are more proficient in Spanish than in English. Schools with Spanish-dominant students have the unique responsibility of providing this group of students with special oral English language instruction. Unfortunately, few elementary school teachers are skilled in oral language development. Most education professors do not understand the importance of oral language development methodology. First year teachers cannot be held accountable for not being competent in oral language instruction if their university professors did not expose them to this instructional method.

Linguistics is the scientific study of language and is of special concern to educators who specialize in bilingual education because linguistics provides teachers with unique insights into language usage and the reasons that children speak a language in a particular manner.

Some of the concepts discussed in this section are: (a) grammar, (b) phonology, (c) idioms, (d) pronunciation, (e) speech, (f) language barriers, (g) language loyalty, (h) American dialects, (i) language and ethnicity, (j) second language instruction, (k) American Indian languages, (l) New World Spanish, (m) linguistics problems of Hispanic children, (n) psycholinguistics, (o) sociolinguistics, (p) geolinguistics, (q) linguistic theory, (r) contrastive linguistics, (s) Puerto Rican Spanish, (t) the psychology of language, and (u) linguistically different learners.

247. ANDERSON, Wallace L. , and Norman C. Stageberg (editors). Introductory Readings on Language, New York: Holt, Rinehart and Winston, 1975. Discussed are such subjects and topics as linguistics, sociolinguistics, psycholinguistics, nonverbal communication, ononatology, and the origin of language, Soft cover. Length: 474 pages.

248. ARLOTTO, Anthony. Introduction to Historical Linguistics. Washington, D.C.: University Press of America, 1981. Discussed are: (a) sound and grammar changes, (b) human culture, (c) human behavior, and (d) the classification of languages. This work is designed to be an introductory text.

249. "A Battle in Any Language," no author. Newsweek, Volume 96, (December 15, 1980), pages 93-94. The anonymous author mentions that sex education, prayer in the public schools, and bilingual education are three

school issues which continue to generate a great deal of controversy. The
reasons for opposition to American bilingual education are discussed.

250. BEBERFALL, Lester. "Some Linguistic problems of the Spanish-
      Speaking People of Texas," Modern Language Journal, Volume 42 (Feb-
      ruary 1958), pages 87-90. The social and linguistic problems of His-
panic Americans who reside in Texas are discussed.

251. BURT, John R. From Phonology to Philology: An Outline of Descriptive
      and Historical Spanish Linguistics. Washington, D.C.: University
      Press of America, 1980. Some features of this 208 page book are: (a)
a bilingual glossary of linguistic terminology, (b) a history of the Spanish language, and (c) the contemporary phonology and morphology of Spanish.

252. CARDENAS, Daniel. Applied Linguistics -- Spanish. Boston: D. C.
      Heath and Company, 1961. A quality book for the beginning linguistics
      and bilingual education major.

253. CARROLL, John B. "Current Issues in Psycholinguistics and Second-
      Language Teaching," TESOL Quarterly, Volume 5, No. 2 (1971), Pages
      101-104. Psycholinguistics may be defined as the effect that psycho-
logical forces or factors have on the manner in which an individual speaks a
language in social situations. An article recommended for the teacher of
Spanish-dominant students who wants to understand the role of psycholinguistics in second language learning.

254. CATTO, Henry E. "Our Language Barriers," Newsweek, Volume 96
      (December 1, 1980), page 25. The author points out that though being
      bilingual or multilingual is a benefit and a mark of sophistication, the
American tradition of having immigrants put aside their language and learn
English is unwisely being abandoned.

255. CELORIO, Marta, and Annette C. Barlow. Handbook of Spanish Idioms.
      Regents Publishing Company, 1973. An idiom is an expression used
      by the people of a given geographic area or cultural group. The authors
book of idioms is for the Spanish professor and the serious student of Spanish.

256. DALBOR, John B. Spanish Pronunciation. New York: Holt, Rinehart,
      and Winston, 1969. For the student of Spanish who wants to perfect
      his or her Spanish language pronunciation.

257. DE VITO, Joseph. The Psychology of Speech and Language: An Intro-
      duction to Psycholinguistics. Washington, D.C.: University Press of
      America, 1981. For the university student taking an introductory
course in psycholinguistics or for the educator interested in speech, language
and human behavior.

258. DURAN, Richard P. (editor). Latino Language and Communicative Be-
      havior. Norwood, New Jersey: Ablex Publishing Corporation, 1981.
      A book of readings which can be used for the staff development of tea-
chers who teach bilingual Hispanic students. Some concepts discussed are:
(a) sociolinguistics, (b) codeswitching, (c) language attitudes, and (d) bilingual
mother-child discourse.

259. EPSTEIN, Noel. Language, Ethnicity, and the Schools. Washington,
      D.C.: Institute for Educational Leadership, The George Washington
      University, 1977. This 104-page book should prove beneficial to

educators, educational policymakers and citizens interested in understanding the rationale for American bilingual education.

260. ESTARELLAS, Juan. Psycholinguistics and the Teaching of Foreign Languages. Spain: Ediciones Anaya, 1971. For the bilingual education educator who wants to comprehend the relationship between psychology and second language learning.

261. FERGUSON, Charles A. (editor). Language in the U.S.A. New York: Cambridge University Press, 1981. A collection of twenty-three articles on the language situation in the United States. Discussed are: (a) language use statistics, (b) bilingualism, (c) New World Spanish, and (d) American Indian languages. This work presents a comprehensive and clear picture of the linguistic picture in the United States.

262. FISHMAN, Joshua. "Bilingual Education in Sociolinguistic Perspective," 1970. ERIC Microfiche, ED 040 404. Fishman's publication explains the relationship between sociolinguistics and bilingual education. For the graduate student of bilingual education. This work also can be found in TESOL Quarterly, Volume 4 (1970), pages 221-222.

263. FISHMAN, Joshua (editor). Language Loyalty in the United States. The Hague: Mouton and Company, 1966. Language loyalty may be defined as the devotion or emotional attachment that a group of people have to their first or home language. One reason that many Hispanic Americans are reluctant to "forget" the Spanish language is that they are very attached to the Spanish language and the Hispanic culture. For the bilingual education graduate student.

264. GREEN, Jerald R. Spanish Phonology for Teachers: A Programmed Introduction. Philadelphia: The Center for Curriculum Development, Inc., 1970. Phonology is the study of the history and evolution of speech sounds and speech patterns used in a given language. Green's book is concerned with Spanish phonology and should appeal to the bilingual education major who wants to better understand the sound structure of the Spanish language.

265. GUMPERZ, John. "On the Linguistic Markers of Bilingual Education," Journal of Social Issues, Volume 23, No. 2 (1967), pages 48-58. A quality article filled with useful information concerning the role of linguistics in bilingual education.

266. HAUGEN, Einar, and Morton Bloomfield. Language as a Human Problem. New York: W. W. Norton and Company, 1973. Most human beings seldom consider how complicated the learning of a language actually is, perhaps because most persons seem to effortlessly learn the language spoken by their parents. This book discusses many of the problems inherent in language acquisition.

267. HESS, Karen, and John Maxwell. "What to Do About Nonstandard Dialects: A Review of the Literature," 1969. ERIC Microfiche, ED 041 027. What should educators do when they find that some of their students do not speak a standard dialect of English, Spanish, or French? Should students be discouraged from speaking nonstandard dialects? For the bilingual education practitioner and the foreign language teacher.

268. HORN, Thomas D. (editor). Readings for the Disadvantaged: Problems of Linguistically Different Learners. New York; Harcourt, Brace and World, Inc., 1970. A book or readings which discusses the language problems of students who are linguistically disadvantaged. Recommended for the bilingual education major.

269. HYMES, Dell. Foundations in Sociolinguistics: An Ethnographic Approach. Philadelphia, Pennsylvania: University of Pennsylvania Press, 1974. A text for the graduate student in linguistics or bilingual education who wants a better understanding of the relationship between language learning and the community in which the language learner resides.

270. _____ (editor). Languages in Culture and Society: A Reader in Linguistics and Anthropology. New York: Harper and Row, 1964. Discussed are the relationships between anthropology, linguistics, culture, and society and how these factors affect human language.

271. JAKOBOVITS, L. A. Foreign Language Learning: A Psycholinguistic Analysis of the Issues. Rowley, Massachusetts: Newbury House, 1970. The author discusses the interrelationships between psychology and foreign language learning.

272. KINTSCH, Walter. "Interlingual Interference and Memory Processes," Journal of Verbal Learning and Verbal Behavior, Volume 8 (1969), pages 16-19. The author discusses the effect of language interference on a bilingual person's memory. An article for the linguistics researcher.

273. LADO, Robert. "Comparison of the Sound System of English and Spanish," Hispania, Volume 33 (March 1956), pages 26-29. Lado, a nationally known English and Spanish language expert, has written an important article on phonology for the bilingual education specialist who wants to compare the sound systems of English and Spanish.

274. _____. Linguistics Across Cultures: Applied Linguistics for Language Learners. Ann Arbor: The University of Michigan Press, 1960. The author's book should appeal to the educator who wants to understand how the principles of linguistics can be applied to living languages.

275. LAIRD, Charlton, and Robert M. Gorrell. Reading About Language. New York: Harcourt, Brace and Jovanovich, Inc., 1971. A collection of readings about various aspects of language. Each article in this book was carefully chosen by the editors. Recommended for linguistics and language majors. Soft cover.

276. LAMB, Rose. Linguistics in Proper Perspective. Columbus, Ohio: Charles E. Merrill Publishing Co., 1967. A book which will give the reader a clear description of the role of linguistics in today's society.

277. LAMBERT, Wallace E. Language, Psychology, and Culture: Essays by Wallace E. Lambert. Stanford, California: Stanford University Press, 1972. A collection of essays by an expert on bilingualism which can be used as a supplementary textbook by linguists, sociologists, and educators who teach bilingual education graduate courses.

278. _____. "Psychological Approaches to the Study of Language, Part I: On Learning, Thinking and Human Abilities," Modern Language Journal, Volume 47 (1963), pages 51-62. Wallace discusses human language

and such related concepts as the psychology of language learning, mental abilities, and the development of the thought process.

279. _____. "Psychological Approaches to the Study of Language, Part II: On Second Language Learning and Bilingualism," <u>Modern Language Journal</u>, Volume 47, (1963), pages 114-119. Discussed are: (a) bilingualism, (b) psychological aspects of language, (c) second language learning, and (d) psychological factors inherent in learning a weaker language.

280. LANGACKER, Ronald W. <u>Language and Its Structure, Some Fundamental Concepts</u>. New York: Harcourt, Brace, Jovanovich, 1968. An excellent basic text for undergraduate linguistics majors and for bilingual education graduate students.

281. LEVINE, Helene F. "Linguistic and Paralinguistic Changes in Spanish-Speakers Learning English," <u>English Language Teaching</u>, Volume 25 (June 1971), pages 288-296. A "must" article for the bilingual education major who has a special interest in the linguistic aspects of bilingual education. The author discusses the subtle and the not so subtle changes which occur in Spanish-dominant persons who are becoming stronger in the English language.

282. MACKEY, W. F. <u>Three Concepts for Geolinguistics</u>. Quebec, Canada: International Center for Research on Bilingualism, 1973. Linguistics is an important component of bilingual education. One "branch" of linguistics is geolinguistics, which is the study of the relationship between language and geography. A research oriented publication which will be of special interest to professors of linguistics.

283. MALMSTROM, Jean, and Annabel Ashley. <u>Dialects, U.S.A.</u> Champaign, Illinois: National Council of Teachers of English, 1963. For the linguistics aficionado who has a special interest in American dialects.

284. MILLER, George A., and Frank Smith (editors). <u>The Genesis of Language: A Psycholinguistic Approach</u>. Cambridge, Massachusetts: The M.I.T. Press, 1966. A technical publication which is a collection of articles on the origin of human language. Soft cover.

285. MILLER, J. Dale. "1,000 Spanish Idioms," 1970. ERIC Microfiche, ED 047 575. An idiom is an expression or phrase which is characteristic of a particular people, region, or nation. In this publication, Miller has compiled 1,000 Spanish language idioms which should prove invaluable to the professor of Spanish.

286. MONTAÑEZ, Lucrecia Casiano. <u>La Pronunciación de los Puertorriqueños en Nueva York</u>. Colombia: Ediciones Tercer Mundo, 1975. It is a recognized fact that different national groups tend to develop a distinctive style of pronouncing many of the words of their national language. For example, Americans, South Africans, Australians, and Englishmen each have developed a distinctive English language pronunciation style; distinct pronunciation styles also exist among the national and cultural groups that speak the Spanish language. Mexicans, Spaniards, Cubans, and Puerto Ricans each have developed their own recognizable Spanish pronunciation style. Montañez has written a work which describes the Spanish pronunciation system of Puerto Ricans in New York City. Written in Spanish.

287. NASH, Rose. <u>Comparing English and Spanish: Patterns in Phonology</u>
<u>and Orthography.</u> New York: Regents Publishing Co. , 1977. A text
for the student of bilingual education desiring to learn about the sound
structure and the spelling system of the Spanish language.

288. _____ (editor). <u>Readings in Spanish-English Contrastive Linguistics.</u>
Hato Rey, Puerto Rico: InterAmerican University Press, 1973. The
Spanish and English languages are compared in this scholarly linguistics
reader. A text for the Spanish language major and for the Linguistics professor.

289. ORNSTEIN, Jacob. "Language Varieties Along the U. S. -Mexican Border, " 1969. ERIC Microfiche, ED 032 520. The United States-Mexican
border stretches across the states of California, Arizona, New Mexico,
and Texas -- from the Pacific Ocean to the Gulf of Mexico. There are various
varieties of Spanish and English spoken along this expansive border; Ornstein's
publication discusses these language dialects.

290. _____. "Report on a Project to Apply Sociolinguistic Research Findings to Educational Needs of Mexican American Bilinguals/Biculturals, "
1972. ERIC Microfiche, ED 077 296. Sociolinguistics may be defined
as the study of the characteristics of language forms and language speakers
in a given region or community. Ornstein maintains that sociolinguistic principles can be used to meet the educational needs of Hispanic bilingual students.

291. PEI, Mario. <u>Glossary of Linguistic Terminology.</u> New York: Doubleday & Co. , 1966. This work is basically a dictionary of linguistic terms
and is an ideal reference tool for students of linguistics and bilingual
education. Paperback.

292. REYES, Donald J. "The Relative Development of Spanish and English as
Abstract and Conceptual Languages in Bilinguals, " 1973. ERIC Microfiche, ED 083 880. As children develop concepts (i. e. , cat, house, candy,
apple, etc.) in a particular language, they gradually become stronger in that
language. Reyes discusses concept development in Spanish-English bilinguals.

293. ROSENQUIST, Carl M. "Why I Speak Spanish, " <u>Texas Foreign Language</u>
<u>Association Bulletin</u>, Volume 5, No. 4 (December 1963). The reader
is provided with a rationale for learning to speak Spanish. For the non-
Spanish monolingual who is seriously considering mastering the Spanish Language.

294. ROSSI-LANDI, Ferruccio. <u>Ideologies of Linguistic Relativity.</u> The
Hague: Mouton, 1973. The author has written a linguistics text which
is concerned with the concepts of linguistic relativity. Recommended
for graduate students in linguistics and bilingual education.

295. ROULET, Eddy. <u>Linguistic Theory, Linguistic Description and Lan-</u>
<u>guage Teaching.</u> London: Longman Group Limited, 1976. The work
attempts to apply linguistic theory to the teaching of foreign languages.

296. SAPORTA, Sol. "Problems in the Comparison of the Morphemic System
of English and Spanish, " <u>Hispania</u>, Volume 39 (March 1956), pages 36-
38. A morpheme is a word or part of a word that conveys meaning and
which cannot be further divided into smaller units to convey meaning. For example, "flyer" is composed of two morphemes: "fly" and "er. " Saporta's

article discusses the problems inherent in comparing the English and Spanish language morphemic systems.

297. SEBEOK, T. (editor). Current Trends in Linguistics. The Hague: Mouton, 1968. Though this text was written in the 1960's, many of the trends mentioned are still apropos.

298. SPOLSKY, Bernard. "Some Psycholinguistic and Sociolinguistic Aspects of Bilingual Education," 1968. ERIC Microfiche, ED 028 412. To thoroughly understand bilingualism and bilingual education, a person must possess at least a rudimentary understanding of linguistics--particularly psycholinguistics and sociolinguistics. Spolsky's publication attempts to provide the reader with a basic grasp of the psycholinguistic and sociolinguistic principles which are applicable to bilingual education.

299. _____. The Language Education of Minority Children. Rowley, Mass. : Newbury House Publisher, Inc. , 1972. This text is for the teacher who wants new ideas on how to teach language to minority group students.

300. STERN, H. Languages and the Young Child. London: Oxford University Press, 1969. A scholarly book on how children acquire language.

301. STOCKWELL, Robert P. , and J. D. Bowen. The Sounds of English and Spanish. Chicago: University of Chicago Press, 1965. The authors compare the English language and Spanish language sound systems. For the bilingual education undergraduate enrolled in a linguistics course.

302. _____, and John W. Martin. The Grammatical Structures of English and Spanish. Chicago: University of Chicago Press, 1965. The author's compare the English language and Spanish language grammatical systems. For the linguistics undergraduate.

303. WALLWORK, J. F. Language and Linguistics: An Introduction to the Study of Language. London: Heinemann Educational Books, 1970. A basic introductory book for the teacher of bilingual children who wants to understand the basic nature of language.

304. WIEDEMER, Jack. "Speak It or Not? Tactics of Language," IDRA Newsletter, (January 1982), page 2. Intercultural Development Research Association, 5835 Callaghan Road, San Antonio, Texas 78228. The author stresses that it is a source of strength for a person to be able to speak a foreign language and a weakness to not speak another nation's language. Citizens of the United States no longer can afford the luxury of being monolingual.

305. YOUNG, Rodney H. "The Question of Linguistic Deficiency in the Bilingual Setting," 1973. ERIC Microfiche, ED 183 879. Many educators maintain that the economically disadvantaged American bilingual child's main educational problem is the child's limited language acquisition in two languages. This and other educational problems are discussed.

VII

SOCIOCULTURAL AND
PSYCHOLOGICAL PERSPECTIVES

This section is concerned with the societal, cultural and psychological aspects of American bilingual-bicultural education. The United States of America is a culturally pluralistic-or multicultural-society. American society has been strengthened by the cultural contributions of groups such as the Japenese, the Chinese, the Poles, the Germans, the Africans, The Irish, and the Hispanics. The cultural diversity found in American society should be nurtured because existing cultural differences in America do not conflict with the primary values and norms of America's dominant culture. Generally, cultural pluralism is perceived as a national asset. It is essential for a society to understand how diverse cultures interact, affect, and strengthen the cultural ways of a society.

The most logical and persuasive argument in support of bilingual education which this writer has heard is that it is based on "sound psychology." Even the staunchest opponents of bilingual education realize that the psychology which reinforces the philosophy of bilingual education cannot be refuted. The psychological is one of the most important components of bilingual education because numerous psychological principles give irrefutable credibility to those who are in favor of providing a bilingual education to both non-English-dominant students. Fortunately, rationality and truth are on the side of bilingual education.

The references in this section cover such topics as: (a) cultural differences, (b) cultural conflict, (c) cultural pluralism, (d) the melting pot theory, (e) cultural values, (f) Puerto Rican youth, (g) undocumented school children, (h) multicultural education, (i) the psychology of bilingualism, (j) ethnic esteem, (k) the self-concept, (l) personality development, (m) bicognitive development, (n) identity crises, and (o) cultural marginality.

306. ABRAHAMS, Roger D. "Cultural Difference and the Melting Pot Ideology," Educational Leadership, (November 1971), pages 118-121. Many
        educational sociologists maintain that the "melting pot theory" is not
working in the United States as well as it once did. In this scholarly piece,
the author discusses various aspects of the melting pot doctrine.

307. _____, and R. C. Troike. Language and Cultural Diversity in American Education. New Jersey: Prentice-Hall Inc., 1972. Teachers must
        prepare themselves for the challenges of teaching linguistically and culturally diverse students. This work is tailor-made for teachers in culturally
pluralistic classrooms who feel inadequately prepared to deal with students
from different cultural backgrounds.

308. ACUÑA, Rudolph. Cultures in Conflict. New York: Charter School
        Books, Inc., 1970. The author is a nationally recognized Hispanic author.
        This work is for the student of educational sociology who wants to understand the causes of cultural conflict in our nation and in our schools.

309. AXELROD, Herman C. Bilingual Background and Its Relation to Cer-
      tain Aspects of Character and Personality of Elementary School Child
      ren. New York: Arno Press, 1978. This text should appeal to the
educator interested in determining how bilingualism, character, and personality are interrelated in the elementary school child.

310. BANKS, James A. "Cultural Pluralism and Contemporary Schools,"
      Integrated Education, Volume 14 (January 1976), pages 32-36. Many
      of our large city public schools are becoming multicultural in student
composition. Teachers no longer can neglect the culture and language of
the culturally different student. Bank's article gives the reader a sound
introduction to the concept of "cultural pluralism."

311. _____. "Cultural Pluralism and the Schools," Educational Leader-
      ship, Volume 32 (December 1974), pages 163-166. The author, an
      expert on multiculturalism, defines cultural pluralism and describes
the public schools' responsibility in providing an adequate education for
multicultural student populations.

312. BONILLA, Eduardo Seda. "Cultural Pluralism and the Education of
      Puerto Rican Youth," Phi Delta Kappan, Volume 53, No. 5 (January
      1972), pages 294-296. Some of the conclusions in this article are
applicable to Mexican American youth.

313. BROWN, Ina C. "What is Valued in Different Cultures," Educational
      Leadership, Volume 27, No. 2 (1969), pages 151-154. Though most
      people, regardless of their cultural group membership, tend to share
similar values, there are differences in values among cultural groups. The
author discusses social values in different cultures. Recommended reading
for educators who teach minority group students.

314. CORTÉZ, Albert, and Sharon Sepulveda-Hassell. "Supreme Court
      Rules in Favor of Education of Undocumented Children," IDRA News-
      letter, (August 1982), pages 3, 5. Intercultural Development Research
Association, 5835 Callaghan, San Antonio, Texas 78228. On June 15, 1982,
The U.S. Supreme Court ruled that to deny a public school education to a
disadvantaged group of undocumented children in Texas would result in their
being permanently locked into the lowest socioeconomic class in America
due to poverty, racial prejudice and inability to speak English.

315. CRAIG, Robert P. "'Multicultural Education,' A Need for Conceptual
      Clarification," Educational Considerations, Volume 9, No. 2 (Spring
      1982), pages 2-4. Some concepts discussed are: (a) the "melting
pot" approach, (b) cultural pluralism, (c) cultural values, and (d) multicultural instruction.

316. ESPINOZA, Marta. "Cultural Conflict in the Classroom," 1971. ERIC
      Microfiche, ED 054 669. Espinoza discusses such topics as: (a) neg-
      ative attitudes toward the Mexican American culture and language, (b)
dropoutism, (c) feelings of alienation, (d) teacher insecurity, and (e) motivation of Spanish-speaking students.

317. EWING, Kern. "The Mexican-American Value System in an Urban En-
      vironment," 1970. ERIC Microfiche, ED 049 860. Social values are
      things in a society which are important to a person. Ewing's publication
discusses the viability of the Mexican American's social values in our nation's

urban centers. Teachers who do not understand how a student's value system affects his school achievement will profit from reading Ewing's publication.

318. GLASSER, William. Schools Without Failure. New York: Harper and Row, 1969. The author clearly proves that once a child receives the label of failure and begins perceiving himself as a failure, the child rarely will succeed in school. (See the effect of failure on page 97 of Glasser's book.) This work should be required reading for all future teachers of Spanish-speaking children.

319. GREELEY, A. M. Why Can't They Be Like Us? New York: E. P. Dutton & Company, 1971. The author provides an excellent explanation of the acculturation process and a lucid description of the various steps of assimilation which an American immigrant passes through before he or she is Americanized. Greeley's work should be required reading for all bilingual education majors because it provides the reader with an appreciation of the problems of American immigrants and their children.

320. HAKES, David T. "Psychological Aspects of Bilingualism," The Modern Language Journal, Volume 49, No. 4 (April 1965). Cited are the effects of being bilingual on a person's psyche. This article provides a serious discussion on the psychology of bilingualism.

321. HUFSTEDLER, Shirley M. "On Bilingual Education, Civil Rights and Language Minority Regulations," NABE Journal, Volume 5, No. 1 (Fall 1980), pages 63-69. Discussed are: (a) the 3.5 million limited English-speaking children in the United States, (b) language rights, (c) the Lau vs. Nichols case, and (d) language suppression.

322. KRALL, Florence R. , and Andrew Gitlin. "Promoting Cultural Awareness Through Ethnography," The Elementary School Journal, Volume 82, No. 4 (March 1982), pages 361-366. The authors define ethnography as a procedure of direct personal observation by which cultural anthropologists study societies and cultures. By acting as ethnographer, students and teachers can obtain a deeper appreciation of other cultural groups.

323. KURALT, Charles A. "The Melting Pot Doesn't Work, Thank God!" Family Circle, (July 1976), pages 81-83. The melting pot theory was accepted in the United States for most of the nation's history. Then in the 1960's it became clear to many educators that many citizens were opposed to the theory of making all Americans into "Anglo Saxons." An article for teachers who teach in a multicultural classroom.

324. LATIMER, Betty. "No One Model American," Journal of Teacher Education, Volume 24 (Winter 1973), pages 264-265. The author stresses that we should not have preconceptions of how a model American or how a model student is supposed to behave or look. For the educator assigned to a pluralistic school.

325. LEVINE, Elaine Sue. Ethnic Esteem Among Anglo, Black and Chicano Children. San Francisco: R&E Research Associates, 1976. An ethnic esteem study about how three different ethnic groups perceive themselves. This study should appeal to the student doing graduate work in the psychology of ethnic groups. Soft cover.

326. LE VINE, R. A. "Parental Goals: A Cross Cultural View," Teachers College Record, Volume 76, No. 2 (1974), pages 226-239. The author

compares the goals of parents from different cultures and how parental
goals can affect the academic achievement of students. The reader who wants
to better understand the term "cross-culture" will want to review this article.

327. MANDERA, Franklin R. An Inquiry Into the Effects of Bilingualism on
Native and Non-Native Americans Viewed in Sociopsychological and
Cultural Terms. New York: Arno Press, 1978. Discussed are: (a)
bilingual literacy, (b) cultural hybrid, (c) marginality, (d) personality development, and (e) the Americanization process. This educational study is a
published doctoral dissertation. Length: 157 pages.

328. MERCADO, Edward. "What Price Inglés," Civil Rights Digest, Volume
3 (Summer 1970), pages 32-35. Spanish-speaking students who are
forced to forget their home language by an English-speaking society
sometimes pay a heavy psychological price. A high priority article for teachers of Hispanic students.

329. PULTE, William. "Are Bilingual-Bicultural Programs Socially Divi-
sive?" The Education Digest, (May 1979), pages 55-57. The author,
an anthropologist, discusses how the transfer principle of learning is
applied in bilingual education programs. Also discussed are: (a) ethnic identity, (b) initial reading instruction, (c) a culturally pluralistic curriculum, and
(d) native culture.

330. RAMÍREZ, Manuel. "Cognitive Styles and Cultural Democracy in Education," Social Science Quarterly, Volume 53, No. 4 (March 1973),
pages 895-904. A cultural democracy is a society where all cultures
are allowed and encouraged to thrive. The author discusses cultural democracy
and the importance of realizing that children have distinct thinking and learning
styles.

331. _____. "Effects of Cultural Marginality on Education and Personality,"
1970. ERIC Microfiche ED 056 805. Many students are attempting to
successfully exist in two cultures. For some students, living in two
cultures is a simple feat but for other students, the endeavor is devastating.
An article for teachers of minority culture students.

332. _____. "Identity Crisis in the Barrios," Music Education Journal,
Volume 56 (May 1970), pages 69-70. Many students have a strong need
to know themselves and their cultural membership. Music can be one
way of helping students find their cultural membership.

333/4. _____., and Alfredo Castañeda. Cultural Democracy, Bicognitive Development, and Education, Volume 36 No. 5 (1972), pages 513-519. When
a teacher is a member of one cultural group and the majority of his or her
students are members of another cultural group, can conflict be far behind?
Though a teacher's attitude toward other cultures has an effect on whether
cultural conflict will occur in a given classroom, other factors have an influence
on whether classroom cultural conflict will occur. Highly recommended reading
for monolingual teachers who teach in a multicultural school.

335. SMITH, William L. "Closing the Lid on the Melting Pot," Phi Delta Kappan,
Volume 53 (January 1972), pages 265-284. Some educators and sociologists are opposed to the melting pot approach whereby all American citizens are turned into English-speaking Americans who behave in one "standardized" way. Smith presents his viewpoint on a controversial social issue.

336. SOARES, Louise M. "Self-Concepts of Disadvantaged and Advantaged Students," Child Study Journal, Volume 1 (Winter 1970), pages 69-73. In this self-concept study, the researcher concludes that Mexican American students do not perceive themselves negatively. Instead, it is the Anglo American group that perceives the Mexican American group in negative ways and consequently the Anglo American group assumes that Mexican Americans perceive themselves in the same light.

337. TRUEBA, Henry T., and Grace P. Guthrie (editors). Culture and the Bilingual Classroom: Studies in Classroom Ethnography. Rowley, Massachusetts: Newbury House, 1981. Thirteen papers are presented which discuss the subtle and invisible differences evident in most bilingual classrooms. Some concepts discussed in this reader are: (a) cultural diversity, (b) classroom observation, (c) ethnography, (d) bilingual education, (e) Hawaiian reading program, (f) the hidden curriculum, and (g) anthropology.

VIII

THE MEXICAN AMERICAN CHALLENGE

Who are the Mexican Americans? Where are the Mexican Americans? How many Mexicans and Mexican Americans reside in the United States of America? How long have the Mexican Americans been in this country? Do they have a history? Do they have a future? Why do Mexicans immigrate to the United States?

There probably are more than ten million Mexican Americans in the United States. Yet, it was not until recently that most English-speaking Americans became aware that the Mexican American people comprise one of the largest minority groups in the nation, because of its high birth rate, the Mexican American people could easily become the nation's largest minority group. For the past forty years, large numbers of Mexican nationals have been entering the United States -- both legally and illegally. Most Mexican immigrants have a limited command of the English language when they migrate to the United States. Besides being unable to communicate effectively in English, most Mexican immigrants possess an extremely limited education. Because most of them in the United States eventually marry and have children, America's public schools currently are facing the serious challenge of educating the Mexican American child of limited English-speaking ability.

The sources in this section will aid educators to better understand the culture, language, and history of the Mexican American school child. Some topics discussed in this section are: (a) the psychological aspects of teaching the Mexican American child, (b) the Mexican American student's educational achievement, (c) the instructional needs of the Mexican American student, and (d) preparing teachers for the Mexican American Child.

338. ACHOR, Shirley. Mexican-Americans in a Dallas Barrio. Tuscon: University of Arizona Press, 1978. Many demographers believe that approximately ten percent of the population of Dallas, Texas is Hispanic, mostly Mexican American. A significant percentage of Dallas' Mexican Americans are either illegal aliens or the sons and daughters of illegal aliens. A large percentage of Dallas' Mexican Americans live in barrios. A small percentage of Dallas' Mexican Americans live in middle class neighborhoods. Social workers and educators employed in large American cities in the Southwest will profit from reading this book.

339. ADKINS, Patricia G. "An Effective Classroom Climate for Mexican-American Students," Education, Volume 92 (December 1971), pages 26-27. Covers such topics as language problems, teacher expectations, teacher attitudes, self-concept of students, and bilingual children's needs.

340. AGUIRRE, Rueben E. Teaching the Chicano/Mexican American Cultural Heritage in the Elementary School: A Teacher's Guide Part I and Part II. San Francisco: R&E Research Associates, 1977. A technical text for the scholar doing educational research on ways to include the Mexican American cultural legacy into the elementary school curriculum. Soft cover.

341. ALEXANDER, Louis. "Texas Helps Her Little Latins," The Orange
      Disc, Volume 15 (July-August 1961), pages 22-27. Alexander discusses
      the strategies employed by Mexican Americans and Anglo Americans
to help educationally disadvantaged Hispanic students in Texas before the
advent of Head Start programs. Bilingual education students will want to
read this sensitive article.

342. ALISKY, Marvin. "The Role of the Mexican American in the History
      of the Southwest," 1969. ERIC Microfiche, ED 046 592. The Mexican
      American student of the American Southwest frequently is left with the
impression that his or her cultural group played an insignificant role in the
development of Texas, California, Arizona, New Mexico, and Colorado. The
typical American history book would give the reader the impression that only
English-speaking people contributed to the development of the Southwest.
Alisky's publication attempts to set the historical record straight.

343. ANDERSON, J. B. "Sociological Determinates of Achievement Among
      Mexican-American Students," (no date). ERIC Microfiche, ED 017 394.
      The factors which influence academic achievement among Spanish-speak-
ing students are discussed in this work. Recommended reading for sociology
and education majors who anticipate teaching Mexican American children.

344. _____, and W. H. Johnson. "Stability and Change Among Three Gen-
      erations of Mexican-Americans: Factors Affecting Achievement," Am-
      erican Educational Research Journal, Volume 8, No. 2 (March 1971),
pages 285-307. Listed are the factors which affect academic achievement
among three Spanish-speaking generations. A well documented work.

345. ARIZONA STATE DEPARTMENT OF PUBLIC INSTRUCTION. "Mexi-
      can American Educational Needs: A Report for the State Superintendent
      of Public Instruction," Arizona State Department of Public Instruction,
Pheonix, Arizona, December 13, 1969. ERIC Microfiche, ED 041 691.
Discussed are the shortcomings of many teachers of Mexican American stu-
dents.

346. BALLESTEROS, David. "Meeting Instructional Needs of Chicano Stu-
      dents," NCRIEEO Newsletter, a publication of the National Center for
      Research and Information on Equal Educational Opportunity. Volume
3, No. 3 (January 1973), pages 4-5. The following subjects are discussed:
(a) five purposes of bilingual education, (b) the rationale for bilingual education, (c) language problems of Mexican American students, and (d) recommendations for more Chicano studies.

347. BALLESTEROS, Octavio A. The Effectiveness of Public School Educa-
      tion for Mexican-American Students as Perceived by Principals of Ele-
      mentary Schools of Predominantly Mexican-American Enrollment. San
Francisco: R&E Research Associates, 1976. A published doctoral dissertation which basically is a state-wide study to determine the effectiveness of
public school education in Texas for Mexican American children. Soft cover.

348. BARAL, D. P. Achievement Levels Among Foreign-Born and Native-
      Born Mexican-American Students. San Francisco: R&E Research
      Associates, 1977. This academic study investigates the academic
achievement scores of Mexican American students born in Mexico and the
United States.

349. BARKER, George C. Social Functions of Language in a Mexican-American Community. Arizona: The University of Arizona Press, 1972. For the student of sociolinguistics doing research on the Mexican American family and community.

350. BRUSSELL, Charles B. Disadvantaged Mexican American Children and Early Educational Experience. Austin, Texas: Southwest Educational Development Corporation, 1968. One of the best ways to give disadvantaged children an educational "head start" is to provide them with organized learning experiences as early as the third year of life. Brussell's publication will appeal to teachers in early childhood education programs.

351. BURMA, John H. Mexican-Americans in the United States. Cambridge, Massachusetts: Schenkman Publishing Company, 1970. Burma, one of the first American writers to write in depth about the Mexican American provides a detailed account of the Mexican American's social, economic, and educational problems.

352. _____. Spanish-Speaking Groups in the United States. Detroit: Blaine Ethridge Books, 1974. A 214-page hardcover book about the Mexican American and other significant Hispanic American groups. Discussed are such topics as education, economics, health, the family, religion, values, and attitudes.

353. CARTER, Thomas P. "Mexican Americans: How the Schools Have Failed Them," College Board Review, Volume 43 (Spring 1970), pages 5-11. Carter has written several articles on education for Mexican American students. According to Carter, our public schools are not meeting their unique educational needs. For public school teachers in the Southwest.

354. _____. Preparing Teachers for Mexican American Children. Las Cruces, New Mexico: ERIC Clearinghouse, 1969. For the public school teacher who has Mexican American students in his or her classroom.

355. _____. "The Negative Self-Concepts of Mexican-American Students," School and Society, Volume 96 (March 1968), pages 217-219. In this educational study, the author discovered that Mexican American youth do not perceive themselves more negatively than do their Anglo American peers. An important study.

356. CRESPIN, Benjamin J. "Means of Facilitating Education Sought," Education, Volume 92, No. 2 (November-December 1971), pages 33-37. The author discusses some of the psychological aspects of teaching the Mexican American child.

357. CRITCHLOW, Donald E. (editor). Reading and the Spanish-Speaking Child. Texas State Council of the International Reading Association, 1975. The booklet is composed of five short articles dealing with the teaching of reading to the Mexican American child. Soft cover.

358. DONAHUE, John W. "Between Two Worlds," America, Volume 146 (May 22, 1982), pages 403-404. This article is a review of an autobiography written by a Mexican American who explains how he felt being in an American school unable to speak the school's language of instruction. The autobiographer also gives his views on American bilingual education.

359. DWORKIN, Anthony G. "Stereotypes and Self-Images Held by Native
      Born and Foreign Born Mexican Americans," Sociology and Social
      Research, Volume 49, No. 2 (January 1965). A study to determine
how Americans of Mexican descent see themselves and other ethnic groups.

360. ESTES, Dwain, and David Darling (editors). Improving Educational
      Opportunities of the Mexican American. Austin, Texas: Southwest
      Educational Development Laboratory, 1967. Provides a rationale for
early childhood education for disadvantaged Spanish-speaking students.

361. FARÍAS, Hector, Jr. "Mexican-American Values and Attitudes Toward
      Education," Phi Delta Kappan, Volume 52 (June 1971), pages 602-604.
      Farías discusses the relationship between the social values of Mexican
Americans and their attitudes toward attending school. Also discussed are
home-school cultural conflicts, personality problems, and intellectual performance.

362. FELDER, Dell. "The Education of Mexican-Americans: Fallacies of
      the Monoculture Approach," Social Education, Volume 34 (October
      1970), pages 639-642, 693. Discussed are: (a) cultural differences,
(b) educational problems of Mexican American students, (c) teaching methods,
(d) test scores, and (e) assessment of intellectual abilities.

363. FORBES, Jack D. "Mexican-Americans, A Handbook for Educators,"
      Far West Laboratory for Educational Research and Development, 1967.
      ERIC Microfiche, ED 013 164. Discussed are such subjects as first
language learning, I. Q. tests, middle class concepts, and low-income students.

364. GAINES, John S. "Treatment of Mexican American History in High
      School Textbooks," Civil Rights Digest, Volume 5 (October 1972),
      pages 35-40. Most high school American history books give little re-
cognition to the numerous social contributions made by Mexican Americans
throughout a large segment of our nation's history. Gaines addresses himself to this historical ommission in his provocative article.

365. GÓMEZ, Ernesto, and Roy E. Becker (editors). Mexican American
      Language and Culture: Implications for Helping Professions. San
      Antonio, Texas: Worden School of Social Services, 1979. Discussed
are such concepts as: (a) cultural assessment, (b) language settlement, (c)
cultural factors, (d) Chicano culture, (e) bilingual linguistic blending, and
(f) assimilation. Recommended reading for non-Hispanic teachers of Mexican American students.

366. GONZÁLES, Carlos. An Overview of the Mestizo Heritage: Implica-
      tions for Teachers of Mexican American Children. San Francisco:
      R&E Research Associates, 1976. A mestizo is a biracial individual.
Many Mexican Americans are biracial -- part Mexican Indian and part Spanish -- while others are multiracial. A technical educational study which
should appeal to many Hispanic college professors. Soft cover.

367. GUERRA, Manuel H. "Educating Chicano Children and Youths," Phi
      Delta Kappan, Volume 53, No. 5 (January 1972), pages 313-314. Phi
      Delta Kappan has a reputation for publishing articles of quality and
Guerra's article is no exception. In this piece, the author gives advice to
teachers of Mexican American students on ways to educate them better.

368. _____. "The Mexican-American Child: Problems or Talents?" 1965.
ERIC Microfiche, ED 045 243. Mexican American students, if properly
encouraged by perceptive teachers, will demonstrate that they are as
talented as the students of any other cultural group. This publication will appeal to teachers who are experiencing difficulty in motivating lower class
Mexican American students of the Southwest.

369. HALE, James M. "Effects of Image Enhancement Indoctrination on
the Self-Concept, Occupational Aspiration Level, and Scholastic Achievement of Mexican-American Model Neighborhood Area Students." Unpublished Doctoral Dissertation, East Texas State University, 1972. The
author, in this experimental education study, recommends that assimilation-
ist goals of the school be discouraged because these goals detract from Mexican American students' sense of cultural identity which consequently produces
a low self-esteem in some students.

370. HEFFERNAN, Helen. "Some Solutions to Problems of Students of Mexican Descent," The Bulletin of the National Association of Secondary
School Principals, Volume 39 (March 1955), pages 43-53. Heffernan
stresses that some teachers, in their anxiety to hasten the acquisition of
English in their students, have attempted to supress Mexican American students from speaking Spanish in the classroom and on the playground. Recommended reading for teachers of Spanish-dominant students.

371. HELLER, Celia S. "Chicano is Beautiful," Commonwealth, Volume 91,
(January 23, 1970), pages 454-458. In the same way that "black is beautiful," many Mexican Americans are espousing the idea that being a Mexican American is a fact of which to be justifiably proud. For years, Mexican
Americans in the Southwest directly and indirectly were given the impression
by other ethnic groups that it was a "disadvantage" to be a Mexican American.
Today, many Mexican Americans are saying, "Chicano is Beautiful." For
teachers in a pluralistic classroom.

372. HENDERSON, Ronald W. "Positive Effects of a Bicultural Preschool
Program on the Intellectual Performance of Mexican-American Children,"
1969. ERIC Microfiche, ED 028 827. In this educational study, the
investigator concludes that integrating disadvantaged Mexican American students into classes with advantaged Anglo American students may have a favor-
able effect on the Mexican American students' intellectual development.

373. HENDRICKS, Herbert W. "The Mexican-American Student and Emigrated Values," College Student Journal, Volume 5 (September-October
1971), pages 52-54. Many teachers are not aware that some of the
social values of the Mexican American student are emigrated values -- values
which have been brought from Mexico. An article for all teachers who need
a better understanding of how social values are acquired by students.

374. HEPNER, Ethel M. "Self-Concepts, Values, and Needs of Mexican-
American Underachievers," 1970. ERIC Microfiche, ED 048 954. The
author, in this self-concept study, makes the point that the reasons for
the lack of academic achievement on the part of many Mexican American students are not readily admissible or adequately understood by teachers and
school administrators. Discussed are such topics as cultural norms, cultural
values, and cultural behavior.

375. _____. "The American Elementary School Versus the Values and Needs
of Mexican-American Boys. Final Report," 1971. ERIC Microfiche,
ED 052 860. The author makes the interesting point that some teachers
tend to give higher grades to students who share the teachers' values, and that
some low achievers have few values which coincide with the values of their
teachers or with high achievers. Grades, the self-concept, and the problems
of the informal classroom also are discussed.

376. HERNÁNDES, Luis. "The Culturally Disadvantaged Mexican-American
Student, Part I," 1967. ERIC Microfiche, ED 020 979. The author contends that most Mexican American Spanish monolingual students are taught
English by teachers who have no awareness of the students' native language or
of the principles involved in teaching English as a second language.

377. HILLERICH, Robert L. "ERMAS: Experiment in Reading for Mexican-
American Students," 1969. ERIC Microfiche, ED 035 526. Described
is a unique reading program specially designed for the Spanish-speaking
Mexican American student. For the school district searching for a more effective reading program for its Hispanic students.

378. HISHIKI, Patricia. "The Self-Concept of Sixth Grade Girls of Mexican-
American Descent," California Journal of Educational Research, Volume
20 (March 1969), pages 56-62. In this educational study, the author compared the self-concept, academic achievement, and intelligence of six-grade
Mexican American girls in selected East Los Angeles schools with similar
variables found in six-grade Anglo American girls in selected Georgia schools.

379. HOFFMAN, Abraham. "Where Are the Mexican Americans? A Textbook Omission Overdue for Revision," The History Teacher, Volume 6
(November 1972), pages 143-150. Most American history books tend to
overlook the Mexican American's role in American history. This informative
piece attempts to deal with this sensitive historical issue which eventually
must be dealt with by social studies teachers.

380. JAKSON, Gregg, and Cecilia Cosca. "The Inequality of Educational
Opportunity in the Southwest: An Observational Study of Ethnically Mixed
Classrooms," American Educational Research Journal, Volume 2 (1974),
pages 219-229. The purpose of this study was to determine whether teachers
behaved differently in their relationship with Anglo American and Mexican
American students.

381. JOHNSON, Henry Sioux, and William J. Hernandez. Educating the Mexican-American. Valley Forge, Pennsylvania: Judson Press, 1970. The
unique educational problems of Mexican American students are discussed.

382. JUSTIN, Neal. "Culture Conflict and Mexican-American Achievement,"
School and Society, Volume 98 (January 1970), pages 27-28. Many educators are not aware that the academic achievement of students can be
affected by cultural shock and by culture conflict. Justin's piece should prove
enlightening to most teachers of Hispanic students.

383. LAMPE, Philip E. Comparative Study of Assimilation of Mexican-Americans: Parochial Schools Versus Public Schools. San Francisco:
R&E Research Associates, 1975. A published doctoral dissertation.
Compares the assimilation of Mexican students in public and parochial
schools. Soft cover.

384. LITSINGER, Dolores Escobar. The Challenge of Teaching Mexican-American Students. Dallas: American Book Company, 1973. Many middle class American educators do not relish the prospect of teaching non-English dominant students because teaching Spanish-dominant students is "hard work." The teaching of non-English dominant students also can be viewed as an exciting professional challenge for today's public and private school teachers. Suggested reference work for teachers in the Southwest.

385. MAZÓN, Manuel Reyes. Adelante: An Emerging Design for Mexican-American Education. Austin, Texas: Center for Communication Research, 1972. Describes an alternate educational program for Mexican American students. For the elementary school principal whose student population is predominantly Mexican American.

386. MEDINA, Rodolfo. "Mexican Americans," Instructor, Volume 81 (January 1972), pages 40-42. First year teachers who have Mexican American students in their classroom but who have a limited understanding of this cultural group will profit from this article about Americans of Mexican ancestry.

387. MEGUIRE, K. H. Educating the Mexican Child in the Elementary School. San Francisco: R&E Research Associates, 1973. For the school administrator who is not satisfied with the education being provided to Mexican American students in his or her school or school district. Soft cover.

388. MEIR, Matt S., and Feliciano Rivera. Dictionary of Mexican American History. Westport, Connecticut: Greenwood Press, 1981. This excellent publication contains terms which will help the teacher in an English-Spanish bilingual education program to understand the unique culture, language and educational needs of Mexican American children. Some terms defined in this dictionary are: (a) bilingual education, (b) biculturalism, (c) Hispano subculture, (d) bilingual legislation, and (e) education. Length: 498 pages. Hardcover.

389. MILLER, Thomas L. "Mexican-Texans at the Alamo," Journal of Mexican American History, Volume 2 (February 1971), pages 33-41. Not all Mexicans at the battle of the Alamo were on the outside shooting in; there were some Mexicans in the Alamo shooting out. In this piece, Miller attempts to set the history of the Alamo straight. For the social studies teacher in a school with a predominantly Mexican American student enrollment.

390. MONTEZ, Phillip. Some Differences in Factors Related to Educational Achievement of Two Mexican-American Groups. San Francisco: R&E Research Associates, 1974. For the educator doing research on the academic achievement of Hispanic students. Soft cover.

391. _____. "Will the Real Mexican American Please Stand Up?" Integrated Education, Volume 8, No. 3, (May-June 1970), pages 43-49. Most English-speaking Americans have had few opportunities to work or socialize with Mexican Americans. Consequently, many misconceptions exist about this ethnic group. Montez has written an important piece about our nation's second largest minority group. Recommended reading for the non-Hispanic teacher of Mexican American students.

392. MONTIEL, Miguel. "The Social Science Myth of the Mexican-American Family," El Grito, Volume 3, No. 4 (Summer 1970). No one can understand and appreciate the Mexican American family as can a Mexican American who is in tune with the Mexican American culture. Or to put it another way, he who sees does not always see it all, especially if he or she is not a member of the group he or she is observing. The author attempts to dispel many of the misconceptions held by non-Hispanics about the Mexican American familia.

393. MOQUIN, Wayne (editor). A Documentary History of the Mexican-Americans. New York: Praeger Publishing Company, Inc. , 1971. Recommended for high school libraries that serve a bilingual Mexican American student population.

394. NAVA, Julián. Mexican Americans: A Brief Look at Their History. New York: Anti-Defamation League of B'nai B'rith, 1970. A booklet for the undergraduate history student contemplating doing graduate work in Mexican American history, history of the Spanish Southwest, or bilingual-bicultural education.

395. _____. The Mexican American In American History. New York: American Book Company, 1973. Nava, a nationally recognized authority on Mexican American history, has produced a work which elaborates on the Mexican American's contributions to our nation's history. A basic text for introductory Chicano history courses or it can be used as a library reference book in high schools that have a bilingual-bicultural education program for Mexican American students.

396. NICHOLL, Larry, and Miguel Gómez. Quality Education for Mexican American Minorities: Sí, Se Puede! -- Yes, It Can Be Done! Washington, D. C. : University Press of America, 1980. This work is a case study in the sociology of education. Examined is the rise and fall of some bilingual education programs in a southern California school district.

397. PALOMARES, Geraldine D. "The Effects of Stereotyping on the Self-Concept of Mexican Americans, " 1970. ERIC Microfiche, ED 056 806. Too many Mexican Americans have been adversely affected by the negative stereotyping which their ethnic group has been accorded throughout the years in this nation. Palomares discusses the effects that negative stereotyping can have on the "group concept" of an ethnic group.

398. PEREZ, Eustolia. "Oral Language Competence Improves Reading Skills of Mexican American Third Graders, " The Reading Teacher, Volume 35, No. 1 (October 1981), pages 24-27. The author contends that Mexican American elementary school children who are not proficient in English need to be provided with English oral language skills development through each of the elementary school grades. The author concludes that a comprehensive program of oral language activities in English will compensate for the inadequate preschool English language experiences of many non-English-dominant Mexican American students.

399. RAMÍREZ, Manuel. "Cultural Democracy: A New Philosophy for Educating the Mexican-American Child, " The National Elementary Principal. Volume 50, No. 2 (November 1970). Each student in the United States has the right to be taught in a school which respects and understands his home culture. In a cultural democracy, a student is taught by

teachers who are sensitive to the needs of culturally diverse students. This piece is for the educator who is searching for a philosophical base for bicult- ural education.

400. _____. , and Clark Taylor. "Mexican-American Cultural Membership and Adjustment to School," in Chicanos: Social and Psychological Per- spectives. St. Louis: C. V. Mosby Company, 1971. The authors dis- cuss the relationship between school adjustment and cultural group identity. The unique learning problems of Mexican American students are mentioned.

401. REYES, Ignacio. A Survey of the Problems Involved in the Americani- zation of the Mexican-American. San Francisco: R&E Research Associates, 1972. Many middle class Americans are of the opinion that too many Mexican Americans are not "melting" quickly enough in the great American melting pot. Reyes' publication discusses the factors which affect the assimilation of Mexican Americans into American society. A technical study. Soft cover.

402. ROWAN, Helen. "A Minority Nobody Knows," The Atlantic, Volume 219, No. 6 (June 1967), pages 47-52. The author provides basic facts and statistics on the Mexican American, a minority which, until recent- ly, most Americans did not realize was such a large and rapidly growing minority group.

403. RUSSELL, Daniel. "Problems of Mexican Children in the Southwest," Journal of Educational Sociology, Volume 17 (December 1943), pages 216-222. Though this article was written during the 1940's, it contains facts which are still useful to teachers of Mexican American children. For example, fourteen cultural characteristics of Mexican American children are discussed.

404. SCHON, Isabel. A Bicultural Heritage: Themes for the Exploration of Mexican and Mexican-American Culture in Books for Children and Adolescents. Metuchen, New Jersey: Scarecrow Press, Inc., 1978. Many school districts in the Southwest want to adopt books which are bicult- ural in orientation. School textbooks which omit the contributions of His- panics are not as relevant in bilingual-bicultural classrooms as those that include the contributions of the Hispanic cultures. This work will help edu- cators to select textbooks appropriate for bicultural students.

405. SCHWARTZ, Audrey James. "A Comparitive Study of Values and Achievement: Mexican-American and Anglo Youth," Sociology of Edu- cation, Volume 44 (Fall 1971), pages 438-462. Do social values affect academic achievement? In this study, the author addresses himself to this frequently asked educational question. For the student of educational sociol- ogy and for the bilingual-bicultural education major.

406. SHERFEY, Richard Wayne. Relationship of Attention Span to Reading Performance in Mexican American Children. San Francisco: R&E Research Associates, 1976. Many reading teachers maintain that the main reason many pupils do not learn to read is due to their weak attention span which is partially caused by a lack of academic motivation. The author's research study is concerned with the effect of attention span on the reading achievement of Mexican American pupils. For the graduate student conduct- ing reading research. Soft cover.

407. SIMMONS, Ozzie G. "The Mutual Images and Expectations of Anglo-Americans and Mexican-Americans," Daedalus, Volume 90 (1961).
For the school counselor conducting research on cultural group perceptions and how these perceptions affect student motivation and achievement.

408. SMITH, Walter E. "Cultural Aspects of Bilingual Education," IDRA Newsletter, (December 1981). Intercultural Development Research Association, 5835 Callaghan, San Antonio, Texas 78228. For the teacher of Mexican American children who wants to know why culture is an integral part of a bilingual education program.

409. SPALDING, Norma. "Learning Problems of Mexican-Americans," Reading Improvement, Volume 7 (February 1970), pages 33-36. The author discusses what she perceives to be the learning problems of Mexican American pupils. Recommended reading for the teacher who has disadvantaged Mexican American children in his or her classroom.

410. STAPLES, Robert. "The Mexican-American Family: Its Modification Over Time and Space," Phylon, Volume 32 (Summer 1971), pages 179-192. Staples discusses the evolution of the Mexican American family. For the bilingual-bicultural education major conducting sociological research on the Chicano family.

411. STEDMAN, James M., and Richard E. McKenzie. "Family Factors Related to Competence in Young, Disadvantaged Mexican-American Children," Part of the Final Report on Head Start Evaluation and Research, 1968-1969. ERIC Microfiche, ED 037 248. A child's linguistic ability, claim the authors, is a highly important learning variable because of its potential relationship to how a teacher perceives the child. The authors stress that a child's linguistic ability constitutes a coping mechanism which often can lead to an easier school adjustment, if high, and a poor school adjustment, if low.

412. STEWART, Ida Santos. "Cultural Differences Between Anglos and Chicanos," Integrated Education, Volume 68 (November-December 1975), pages 21-23. Though many American educators find it unpleasant to discuss cultural differences and similarities among ethnic groups, these differences and similarities are a reality. Stewart has written a piece which should appeal to undergraduate sociology and education majors in the Southwest.

413. TAYLOR, Marie E. "Educational and Cultural Values of Mexican-American Parents: How They Influence the School Achievement of Their Children," 1970. ERIC Microfiche, ED 050 842. This educational study tends to show that Mexican American parents value education and that parental attitudes have a positive influence on the educational achievement of children. The author concludes that the schools need to realize that there exist similarities as well as differences between Anglo American and Mexican American value systems.

414. WELLS, Gladys. Factors Influencing the Assimilation of the Mexican in Texas. San Francisco: R&E Research Associates, 1974. Many Mexican Americans in Texas do not want to forget their Mexican customs and traditions nor do they want to forget the langauge of the "old country" as did many Americans whose parents emigrated from Asian and European nations. Wells' book is for the doctoral student doing research on the sociology of the Mexican American.

415. WITHERS, Charles D. Problems of Mexican Boys. San Francisco:
      R&E Research Associates, 1974. A research study of the social pro-
      blems of Chicano youth. For the social worker who works in the
barrio and the educator assigned to a Chicano school with a bilingual program. Soft cover.

IX

ADMINISTRATION, COUNSELING, TESTING, AND EVALUATION

Whenever bilingual education teachers meet in conferences, seminars and workshops, the following question is asked: "What tests are available for measuring bilingualism in children who enroll in a bilingual education program?" Unfortunately, there presently are few effective assessment instruments to measure language dominance, language level, and language proficiency of bilingual students in America's schools. However, the future looks bright for bilingual student testing because many educators and psychologists currently are diligently working on the development of bilingual assessment instruments.

The success of a bilingual-bicultural education program is largely dependent on the cooperation of school administrators, bilingual education supervisors, school counselors, school psychologists, and bilingual paraprofessionals. The selections in this section should prove useful to the school personnel mentioned above.

Some of the topics discussed below are: (a) bilingual school organizations, (b) bilingual education program staffing patterns, (c) bilingual program evaluation, (d) bilingual program supervision, (e) cross-cultural counseling, (f) minority counseling, (g) group counseling and the Hispanic student, (h) intelligence testing and the Hispanic child, (i) testwiseness of Hispanic children, (j) nonverbal tests for bilingual children, (k) problems of assessing childhood bilingualism, (l) language assessment instruments, (m) oral language tests, (n) teacher aides, and (o) educational accountability.

416. ADLER, Manfred. "Intelligence Testing of the Culturally Disadvantaged," Journal of Negro Education, Volume 37 (Summer 1968), pages 258-267. Adler discusses the validity of administering mental tests to culturally different students. An important article for university students specializing in educational psychology or in multicultural education.

417. ARCINIEGA, Miguel, and Betty J. Newlon. "A Theoretical Rationale for Cross-Cultural Family Counseling," The School Counselor, Volume 29, No. 2 (November 1981), pages 89-96. School counselors who serve students from minority cultures should become familiar with "cross-cultural pluralistic counseling." In this piece, the authors discuss this form of counseling.

418. ATKINSON, G. M., and D. Wing Sue. Counseling American Minorities: A Cross-Cultural Perspective. Dubuque, Iowa: William Brown Company, 1979. The major theme of this book is that any counselor can establish the necessary conditions to be effective with culturally different counselees. Chapters are devoted to the following cultural groups: American Indians, Asian Americans, African Americans, Puerto Ricans, and Mexican Americans.

419. BOCK, Darrell. "Blaming Genes Improper," IDRA Newsletter, (Aug-
      ust 1982), page 4. Intercultural Development Research Association,
      5835 Callaghan, San Antonio, Texas 78228. This newsletter is free
upon request. The author stresses that the average differences in cognitive
test performance between Anglo American, African American and Hispanic
American student populations can be attributed to cultural factors and not to
genetic factors.

420. CHANDLER, John T. "An Investigation of Spanish-Speaking Pupils
      Placed in Classes for the Educable Mentally Retarded, "Journal
      of Mexican American Studies, Volume 1 (February 1970), pages 58-
63. Graduate students doing research on the education of Mexican American
students will want to refer to this piece. Special education teachers in the
Southwest also can profit from reading this article.

421. _____. "Spanish-Speaking Pupils Classified as Educable Mentally
      Retarded," 1969. ERIC Microfiche, ED 050 845. Teachers who do not
      comprehend the difference between "educational retardation" and "men-
tal retardation" will profit from digesting the thoughts in this publication.

422. CLARIZIO, Harvey F. "Intellectual Assessment of Hispanic Children,"
      Psychology in the Schools, Volume 19, No. 1 (1982). Clarizio dis-
      cusses the issue of whether some individual intelligence tests are
biased against Hispanic school children. Stressed is the importance of non-
discriminatory testing for non-Anglo American students.

423. CORTÉZ, Albert. "Minorities and Minimum Competency Testing: A
      Critical Examination of Policy Issues," IDRA Newsletter, (September
      1982), pages 1-2, 4. Intercultural Development Research Association,
5835 Callaghan, San Antonio, Texas 78228. The author discusses how the
minimum competency testing movement may effect the education of culturally
and linguistically different students in American public schools.

424. CRITCHLOW, Donald E. Dos Amigos Verbal Language Scales Manual.
      San Rafael, California: Academic Therapy Publications, 1974. These
      language scales can be used by educators in an English-Spanish bilin-
gual education program.

425. DARCEY, Natalie T. "A Review of the Literature on the Effects of
      Bilingualism Upon the Measurement of Intelligence," Journal of Genetic
      Psychology, Volume 82, No. 1 (1953), pages 21-57. Darcey shares
with the reader her findings concerning the effect that bilingualism has upon
an individual's cognitive ability. Recommended reading for professors of
linguistics and bilingual education. Though this article was published in the
1950's, it still has value in the 1980's.

426. DREISBACH, Melanie, and B. K. Keogh. "Testwiseness as a Factor
      in Readiness Test Performance of Young Mexican American Children,"
      Journal of Educational Psychology, Volume 74, No. 2 (April 1982),
pages 224-229. The authors conclude that testwiseness is an important influence on nonmajority children's test performance and this fact should be
taken into account in readiness assessment programs.

427. EHRLICH, Alan. "Tests in Spanish and Other Languages and Non-Ver-
      bal Tests for Children in Bilingual Programs: An Annotated Bibliogra-
      phy," 1973. ERIC Microfiche, ED 078 713. Some of the tests in this

publication can be administered to students who are entering Spanish-English bilingual education programs.

428. GAARDER, Bruce. "Organization of the Bilingual School," Journal of Social Issues, Volume 23, No. 2 (1967), pages 110-121. How should a bilingual school be organized? Are there various ways to organize a bilingual school program? These and other organizational questions are answered in Gaarder's piece on bilingual school organization. Recommended reading for all school principals and bilingual education program directors who supervise a bilingual education program.

429. GARTH, Thomas R. "The Administration of Non-Language Intelligence Tests to Mexicans," Journal of Abnormal and Social Psychology, Volume 31 (1936), pages 53-58. This is one of the earlier articles about the Mexican child's difficulty with English language intelligence tests.

430. _____. "The Hypothesis of Racial Differences," Journal of Social Psychology, Volume 2 (1937), pages 224-231. The author concludes from his intelligence test studies that intelligence test score differences among students from different racial groups are more attributed to differences in opportunity than to any racial determinant. An old but valid article.

431. GILLIAM, Bettye, and Sylvia C. Peña. "The Fry Graph Applied to Spanish Readability," The Reading Teacher, Volume 33, No. 4 (January 1980), pages 427-430. The authors discuss the use of the Fry Graph to determine the grade level of Spanish language materials.

432. GONZÁLEZ, Juan. "Staffing Patterns in a Bilingual Education Program: The Role of the Monolingual Teacher," The Journal of the National Association for Bilingual Education, Volume 1 (May 1977), page 65. Recommended reading for the school administrator who cannot find enough Spanish-speaking teachers for the bilingual classroom.

433. GUDRIDGE, Beatrice M. Paraprofessionals in Schools: How New Careerists Bolster Education. Washington, D.C.: National School Public Relations Association, 1972. This publication explains how teacher aides can strengthen the typical school program. A detailed explanation of the teacher aide's role in the elementary school classroom is provided. Recommended reading for teacher aides, future teacher aides, and bilingual education program teachers who have a teacher aide in the classroom.

434. HARRIS, David P. Testing English as a Second Language. New York: McGraw-Hill Book Company, 1969. For the educator concerned with ESL (English as a Second Language) evaluation procedures.

435. HERNÁNDEZ-DOMÍNGUEZ, José L., and Donald Gertenback. "Bilingual Education and Accountability: A Perceptual View," 1972. ERIC Microfiche, ED 074 817. Today's educators constantly are hearing and reading that educational accountability has finally arrived -- that teachers and administrators are being held accountable for student progress in the classroom. Bilingual education teachers and administrators should be especially concerned with educational accountability because most American bilingual education programs rely heavily on federal funding and the federal government holds school districts accountable for the wise use of these funds.

436. HOFFMAN, M. The Measurement of Bilingual Background. New York:
    Bureau of Publications, Columbia University, Teachers College, 1934.
    This is one of the earlier publications on the subject of bilingual assess-
ment which should be of value to the researcher compiling a history of bilingualism in America.

437. HOLLOMON, John. "Problems of Assessing Bilingualism in Children
    Entering School." Unpublished Doctor's dissertation. Albuquerque:
    The University of New Mexico, 1973. For the graduate student doing
research on the assessment of bilingualism in Spanish-dominant Mexican
American pupils.

438. HOWARD, Douglas P. "Pitfalls in the Multicultural Diagnostic/Reme-
    dial Process: A Central American Experience," Journal of Multiling-
    ual and Multicultural Development, Volume 3, No. 1 (1982), pages 41-
46. The author concludes that diagnostic and screening devices which are
not developed for and standardized on a particular population, should not be
used with that population unless modifications and adjustments are made.

439. The Initial Screening and Diagnostic Assessment of Students of Limited
    English Proficiency. No author. 1980. Los Angeles: National Dis-
    semination and Assessment Center, California State University, 5151
State University Drive, Los Angeles, California 90032. This fifty-page
guide was written to provide school districts with procedures and resources
for the initial screening and diagnostic assessment of the English language
skills of non-English-dominant school children.

440. JACKSON, S. L. Cross Cultural Attitude Inventory. Austin, Texas:
    Region 13 Education Service Center, 1973. The purpose of this inventory
    is to assess cross cultural attitudes of educators. A useful tool for bi-
lingual education program administrators.

441. _____. "Key Issues in Bilingual Program Evaluation," IDRA Newsletter
    ter, (February 1982), pages 4-6. Intercultural Development Research
    Association, 5835 Callaghan Road, San Antonio, Texas 78228. This
newsletter is free upon request. Three important issues concerning the effectiveness of bilingual education programs are discussed.

442. KITTELL, Jack E. "Bilingualism and Language-Non-Language Intel-
    ligence Scores of Third Grade Children," Journal of Educational Re-
    search, Volume 52, No. 7 (November 1959), pages 263-268. The
author did research on the effects of bilingualism on the intelligence test
scores of bilingual elementary school children. For the research oriented
scholar of bilingual education.

443. LEO, Paul F. "The Effects of Two Types of Group Counseling Upon
    the Academic Achievement and Self-Concept of Mexican-American Pu-
    pils in the Elementary School," 1972. ERIC Microfiche, ED 059 002.
Leo mentions four factors which contribute to the formation of a person's
self-concept: (a) a person's style of responding to devaluation, (b) the history of a person's successes, (c) a person's values and aspirations, and
(d) the amount of respect, acceptance and concerned treatment a person receives from others. Suggested reading for the school counselor assigned
to an English-Spanish bilingual education program.

444. MERCER, Jane R. "Current Retardation Procedures and the Psycho-
    logical and Social Implications on the Mexican-American," 1970. ERIC

Microfiche, ED 052 848. Too many Spanish-speaking children in the public schools of the American Southwest are being erroneously placed in special education classes. The psychological implications of being mistakenly labelled as a mentally retarded child are discussed in Mercer's publication.

445. MOSLEY, W. J. , and H. H. Spicker. "Mainstreaming for the Educationally Deprived," Theory Into Practice, Volume 14 (1975), pages 73-81. This enlightening piece should be read carefully by school superintendents, curriculum directors, and elementary school principals who serve large numbers of lower class minority group pupils.

446. PÉREZ, Carlos V. "Auxiliary Personnel in Bilingual Education," Paper presented at the Fifth Annual TESOL Convention, 1971. ERIC Microfiche, ED 052 648. The author points out that the introduction of auxiliary personnel into a school system may provide more individualized instruction for school children and that auxiliary personnel may serve to link the school and community more closely.

447. PIETROFESA, John J. "Self-Concept: A Vital Factor in School and Career Development," The Clearing House, Volume 44 (September 1969), pages 37-40. The author stresses that the self-concept is an important factor in the career development of individuals. An individual must be able to perceive himself as a skilled worker, technical worker, or professional if he is to eventually belong to one of these groups. For the graduate student specializing in guidance and counseling who plans to serve Hispanic students.

448. PLETCHER, Barbara. Guide to Assessment Instruments for Limited English-Speaking Students. New York: Santillana Publishing Company, 1978. A catalogue which will help the bilingual education teacher to select the correct test for his elementary pupils of limited English-speaking ability. Languages covered in this guide are Spanish, Portuguese, Chinese, French, Italian, Navajo, and Tagalog.

449. RIESSMAN, Frank, and Alan Gartner. "Paraprofessionals: The Effect on Children's Learning," The Urban Review, Volume 4 (October 1969), pages 21-22. What effect do teachers have on the academic achievement of children? The author contends that teacher aides do have a positive effect on children's school achievement. Suggested reading for public school teacher aides and school principals who serve lower class bilingual children.

450. RIVERA, Charlene. "Assessment of the Language Proficiency of Bilingual Persons," Forum, Volume 4, No. 8 (October 1981), pages 3-4. Forum is published monthly by National Clearinghouse for Bilingual Education, 1300 Wilson Blvd. , Suite B2-11, Rosslyn, Virginia 22209. This article is a summary of recommendations made at the Language Proficiency Assessment Synposium held in Warrenton, Virginia on March 14-18, 1981. Note: Forum is free upon request.

451. ROBLEDO, Maria del Refugio. "Bilingual Evaluation Research: Does It Work?" IDRA Newsletter, (February 1982), pages 1-3, 6-7. Intercultural Development Research Association, 5835 Callaghan Road, San Antonio, Texas 78228. The following factors are discussed: (a) the research, (b) the researcher, (c) the information users, and (d) preexisting conditions. Note: IDRA Newsletter is free upon request.

452. RODRIGUEZ, Juan C. Supervision of Bilingual Programs. New York: Arno Press, 1978. This work describes and discusses the implementation and supervision of the Transitional Bilingual Education Act of Massachusetts. This bilingual act can serve as a model for other American states planning to implement a statewide bilingual education program.

453. ROSEN, Pamela. "Tests for Spanish-Speaking Children: An Annotated Bibliography, " 1971. ERIC Microfiche, ED 056 084. This publication should prove invaluable to bilingual education resource teachers who are responsible for testing Spanish-speaking students in an English-Spanish bilingual education program.

454. SILVERMAN, R. J. , and J. K. Noa. Oral Language Tests for Bilingual Students: An Evaluation of Language Dominance and Proficiency Instruments. Center for Bilingual Education, Northwest Regional Educational Laboratory, 1977. This work lists and describes commercially available tests which can be used by schools with bilingual education programs. Length: 142 pages.

455. STANFORD, Madeleine R. "Don't Discard Those I. Q. Tests, " Texas Outlook, Volume 47 (October 1963), page 31. In this brief, perceptive piece, the author advises that teachers of Mexican American students should be encouraged to view I. Q. test results not as indicators of more or less established mental ability but rather as flexible indicators of an expected operational level at a given time. Stanford's article should be required reading for all education majors in the Southwest.

456. THORUM, Arden R. Language Assessment Instruments: Infancy Through Adulthood. Springfield, Illinois: Charles C. Thomas, Publisher, 1981. Chapter 6 of this hardcover book lists and describes the language assessment instruments used in American bilingual education programs. Thirteen different assessment instruments are discussed. An invaluable publication for schools with a bilingual education program.

457. ULIBARRI, Horacio. "Bilingual Education: A Handbook for Educators, " University of New Mexico, 1970. ERIC Microfiche, ED 038 078. The author contends that perhaps the most important point to consider in the selection and implementation of materials for bilingual students is that the materials must be relevant to the educational program. A useful handbook for bilingual education program administrators.

458. UPSHUR, J. , and J. Fata (editors). Problems in Foreign Language Testing. Ann Arbor, Michigan: University of Michigan Press, 1969. This book should be of value to bilingual education program testers and evaluators and to ESL (English as a Second Language) instructors.

459. VALENCIA, Atilano A. "Research and Development Needs and Priorities for the Education of the Spanish-Speaking People, " Southwestern Cooperative Educational Laboratory, Albuquerque, New Mexico, 1970. The author is concerned with the irrelevancy and inappropriateness of present-day instruments in measuring the intelligence of Mexican American children--a fact which needs to be recognized by all institutions, organizations, agencies, and individuals involved in the education of this group of learners.

460. VALETTE, Rebecca M. Modern Language Testing: A Handbook. New York: Harcourt, Brace and World, Inc. , 1967. An outstanding handbook

for the teacher of modern languages (i. e. , German, Spanish, French, Italian, Etc. ,) who needs additional insights into the intricacies of language testing.

461. ZIRKEL, Perry A. "The Why's and Ways of Testing Bilinguality Before Teaching Bilingually," The Elementary School Journal, Volume 76 (March 1976), pages 323-330. The author explains how to determine a student's bilingual status.

X

STUDIES, REPORTS, AND PAPERS

A field of knowledge progresses when professionals in the field contribute knowledge to the field. Three popular ways that professionals contribute are by conducting studies, submitting reports and presenting papers at professional conferences and annual conventions. Because American bilingual education is a relatively new field of knowledge, it is especially important that professionals involved in bilingual education conduct educational studies, submit reports, and present papers. It is fortunate for American bilingual-bicultural education that many talented educators, sociologists, psychologists and linguists are involved in contributing knowledge to the field.

The references in the section are concerned with studies, reports and papers related to the bilingual and bicultural education of children in the United States.

462. ALEXANDER, David J. , and Alfonso Nava. A Public Policy Analysis of Bilingual Education in California. San Francisco: R&E Research Associates, 1976. A technical study on bilingual education in California. For the educational researcher specializing in bilingualism. Soft cover.

463. ANDERSON, Mary. A Comparative Study of the English-Speaking and Spanish-Speaking Beginners in the Public Schools. San Francisco: R&E Research Associates, 1975. An educational study for doctoral students conducting research on the Mexican American child. Soft Cover.

464. ANDERSSON, Theodore. "An Experimental Study of Bilingual Affective Education for Mexican American Children in Grades K and 1," 1970. ERIC Microfiche, ED 056 536. This study was conducted by a nationally known expert on bilingual education who has a reputation for conducting sound experimental studies. Andersson discusses "attitude education" for kindergarten and first grade students in bilingual education programs.

465. ANISFELD, E. "A Comparison of the Cognitive Functioning of Monolinguals and Bilinguals." Unpublished Doctoral Dissertation, McGill University, 1964. Many opponents of bilingual education maintain that bilingualism is an impediment to a child's intellectual development. In this study, Anisfeld attempts to determine if there is a significant difference between the mental functioning of bilinguals and monolinguals.

466. BAKER, K. A. , and A. A. De Kanter. Effectiveness of Bilingual Education: A Review of the Literature. Washington, D.C. : U.S. Department of Education, 1981. A commentary on the state of the art in American bilingual education.

467. BERNAL, Joe J. , and Gloria Zamora. "Bilingual Education Research:

Foundations for Institutionalization," IDRA Newsletter, (September 1981), pages 2-3, 5, 7-8. Intercultural Development Research Association, 5835 Callaghan, San Antonio, Texas 78228. Note: IDRA Newsletter is free upon request. This report attempts to synthesize empirical research regarding bilingual education program effectiveness.

468. BEY, Theresa M. "Parental Viewpoints on Culture and Language," IDRA Newsletter, (March 1982), pages 3-4, 7. Intercultural Development Research Association, 5835 Callaghan Road, San Antonio, Texas 78228. A study which indicates that parents are uncertain about the cultural values being promoted in the schools. Some concepts discussed are: (a) code switching, (b) Black English, (c) standard English, and (d) nonstandard English.

469. CABRERA, Ysidro A. A Study of American and Mexican Culture Values and Their Significance in Education. San Francisco: R&E Research Associates, 1972. Many educators are beginning to understand that a cultural group's social values have an effect on how the group's children fare in school. A technical academic study.

470. CAMPBELL, Russell N., and T. C. Gray. "Critique of the U.S. Department of Education Report on Effectiveness of Bilingual Education: A Review of the Literature," IDRA News letter, (January 1982), pages 3-5. Intercultural Development Research Association, 5835 Callaghan, San Antonio, Texas 78228. The authors stress the need to provide non-English-speaking students the opportunity to learn through two languages with almost no risk to their success in school.

471. CAPLAN, S. W., and R. A. Ruble. "A Study of Culturally Imposed Factors on School Achievement in a Metropolitan Area," The Journal of Educational Research, Volume 58 (September 1964), pages 16-21. In this study, 100 families in a Spanish-speaking community were interviewed to determine if the social values of bilingual parents and monolingual parents differed significantly. Another purpose of this research study was to determine if cultural factors affect the academic success of school children.

472. CARRILLO, Frederico M. The Development of a Rationale and Model Program to Prepare Teachers for the Bilingual-Bicultural Secondary School Programs. San Francisco: R&E Research Associates, 1977. An education research study which describes existing secondary school bilingual education projects for Mexican Americans in Arizona, California, New Mexico and Texas. The study also contains a suggested teacher education program for students majoring in secondary bilingual education.

473. CORNEJO, Richard. A Synthesis of Theories and Research on the Effects of Teaching in First and Second Languages: Implications for Bilingual Education. Austin, Texas: National Educational Laboratory Publichers, no date. An extremely technical publication recommended for the serious researcher of the role of first and second language instruction in American bilingual education programs.

474. DUGAS, Don. "Research Relevant to the Development of Bilingual Curricula," Center for Research on Language and Language Behavior, University of Michigan, 1967. ERIC Microfiche, ED 018 298. In this report, the author stresses that the ideal product of bilingual education is a person who is bicultural and bilingual. The author also contends that children learn more from normal conversation situations than from artificial patterns.

475. DURRETT, M. E., and Florence Pirofski. "A Pilot Study of the Effects of Heterogeneous and Homogeneous Groupings on Mexican-American and Anglo Children Attending Prekindergarten Programs." 1971. ERIC Microfiche, ED 047 862. Many teachers are uncertain whether to group students heterogeneously or homogeneously. This study discusses the effects of different types of grouping on Anglo and Mexican pupils.

476. EDUCATIONAL SYSTEMS CORPORATION. "National Conference on Bilingual Education: Language Skills," The Final Report for Bureau of Research, United States Office of Education, 1969. ERIC Microfiche, ED 033 256. This publication provides an understandable definition and clear explanation of bilingual education.

477. FLORES, Zella K. The Relation of Language Difficulty to Intelligence and School Retardation in a Group of Spanish-Speaking Children. San Francisco: R&E Research Associates, 1975. For the graduate student doing research on bilingualism and the academic achievement of Mexican American students. Soft cover.

478. GALLEGOS, Ruben. "A Comparison Study of Achievement and Adjustment of Mexican-American Migrant and Non-Migrant Children in the Elementary School." Unpublished Doctoral dissertation, East Texas State University, 1970. For the doctoral student doing educational or psychological research on the Mexican American migrant pupil.

479. GALVÁN, Robert Rogers. "Bilingualism as It Relates to Intelligence, Test Scores, and School Achievement Among Culturally Deprived Spanish-American Children." Unpublished Doctoral dissertation, East Texas State University, 1967. For the doctoral student doing educational research on bilingualism or on the Mexican American school child.

480. HARDGROVE, and Hinojosa. Politics of Bilingual Education: A Study of Four Southwest Texas Communities. Machac, Texas: Sterling Swift Publishing Company, 1976. This book should appeal to those readers interested in determining whether bilingual education and community politics are sometimes intertwined. For the politically inclined educator and educational sociologist.

481. HERBERT, Charles H. "Initial Reading in Spanish for Bilinguals," 1971. ERIC Microfiche, ED 061 813. Paper presented at the Conference of Child Language, Chicago, Illinois, November 22-24, 1971. For the teacher in a bilingual classroom who needs more insights into reading instruction methodology for the Hispanic American pupil.

482. HERR, Selma E. "The Effect of Pre-First Grade Training Upon Reading Readiness and Reading Achievement Among Spanish-American Children," The Journal of Educational Psychology, Volume 37 (January 1946), pages 87-102. The purpose of this study was to determine the effect of a year of pre-first-grade training upon the reading readiness and achievement of Spanish-speaking children in the first grade. A dated but informative educational study.

483. HODGE, Marie Gardner. "The Status of Bilingual Education in Texas," Unpublished Master's thesis, North Texas State University, 1971. Hodge discusses the following topics: (a) quality education for Mexican Ameri-

cans in Texas and in the Southwest, (b) history of bilingual education, (c) I. Q. testing, (d) cultural values, (e) cultural awareness, and (f) unfair testing of Mexican Americans.

484. LINTON, Thomas H. "A Study of the Relationship of Global Self-Concept, Academic Self-Concept, and Academic Achievement Among Anglo
and Mexican American Sixth Grade Students," Paper presented at the
annual meeting of the American Educational Research Association, Chicago,
Illinois, April 3-7, 1972. ERIC Microfiche, ED 063 053. This study was
conducted to determine if 172 Anglo American and 160 Mexican American
sixth graders from New Mexico differed significantly in their global and academic self-concepts.

485. MACKEY, William F. , and Theodore Andersson (editors). Bilingualism in Early Childhood Rowley, Massachusetts, 1977. This book is
a collection of conference papers which deal with early childhood, child
language, and bilingualism. Early childhood education teachers who teach
bilingual children will benefit from the thoughts contained in this compilation.
Length: 443 pages.

486. MACMILLAN, Robert Wilson. "A Study of the Effect of Socioeconomic
Factors on the School Achievement of Spanish-Speaking School Beginners,"
Dissertation Abstracts, Volume 27, No. 10 (April 1967), pages 3229-A,
3230-A. This study was conducted to test the correlation between various
socioeconomic variables and the academic achievement of Spanish-speaking
first grade children. The study indicates that the Mexican American students
in the study had a more positive attitude toward education than did the Anglo
American and African American students in the study.

487. MANS, Rolando. "An Experimental Approach to the Teaching of Spanish
at the Primary Level," Master's thesis, Sacramento State College,
1971. ERIC Microfiche, Ed 056 602. According to Mans, The philosophy
of the American educational system is based on the idea of inculcating Anglo
American middle class ideals on all students. This educational philosophy
has led to a depreciation of cultures and languages which are different from
the dominant culture. Also discussed are teacher attitudes, monolingualism,
and cultural values.

488. MCNEIL, Guy Brett. "A Pre-First Grade Oral English Program as
Related to Scholastic Achievement of Spanish-Speaking Children," Dissertation Abstracts, Volume 19 (February-April 1959), page 2551. In
this doctoral dissertation, the investigator points out that the most obvious
handicap of preschool Spanish-speaking children is their inability to speak and
understand the English language. The investigator suggests that the scholastic
achievement of Hispanic students can be dramatically advanced by enrolling
them in a pre-first-grade oral English program.

489. MODIANO, Nancy. "A Comparative Study of Two Approaches to the
Teaching of Reading in the National Language," 1966. ERIC Microfiche,
ED 010 049. Modiano is an internationally recognized bilingual education
researcher. Her specialty is bilingual reading instruction; she has done ex-
tensive reading research in the interior of Mexico. This publication is for the
bilingual education resource teacher who desires to become more knowledgeable in bilingual reading methodology.

490. _____. "National or Mother Language Beginning Reading: A Comparative

Study," Research in the Teaching of Reading, Volume 1 (1968). Should
a student be provided with initial reading instruction in his mother language or in the national language? Modiano shares with the reader her research
findings on this fundamental reading question. Suggested reading for the bilingual education resource teacher.

491. NATIONAL CONSORTIA FOR BILINGUAL EDUCATION. "Report of
     Survey Findings: Assessment of Needs of Bilingual Education Programs, "
     1971. ERIC Microfiche, ED 050 875. The authors of this survey con-
cluded that there is an urgent need to develop relevant materials for students,
teachers and parents involved in American bilingual education programs.

492. OLESINI, José. "The Effects of Bilingual Instruction on the Achieve-
     ment of Elementary Pupils. " Unpublished Doctoral Dissertation, East
     Texas State University, 1971. The results of this educational study in-
dicated that bilingual children of both sexes achieved greater academic curricula gains when they were instructed with bilingual methods. The author con-
cluded that bilingual instruction reduces the language handicap which many
bilingual children encounter at school. A sound study.

493. OLIVER, Joseph D. Los Ojos: A Study of Bilingual Behavior. San
     Francisco: R&E Research Associates, 1975. Many persons familiar
     with bilingual Hispanics maintain that many Hispanics have a distinct
way of using their eyes to express themselves -- a way which may be described
as expressive and sensuous. Social psychologists conducting research on the
human behavior of bilingual Americans will want to review this technical
publication. Soft cover.

494. OVANDO, Carlos Julio. Factors Influencing High School Latino Stu-
     dents' Aspirations to Go to College: The Urban Midwest. San Francisco:
     R&E Research Associates, 1977. Ovando discusses the factors which
cause Hispanic students to strive for a higher education. A technical study
for the graduate student specializing in guidance and counseling. Soft cover.

495. PERALES, Alonzo M. , and Lester B. Howard. "On Teaching the Dis-
     ciplines to Disadvantaged Mexican-Americans, " Paper read at Third
     Annual TESOL Convention, 1969. ERIC Microfiche, ED 031 689. Dis-
cussed are such topics as: (a) the Mexican American's English language
problem, (b) materials and methods for teaching Spanish-dominant students,
(c) language development, and (d) oral language experience.

496. PHILLIPS, Jean M. "Code-Switching in Bilingual Classrooms, " 1975.
     Master's tesis, California State University, ERIC Microfiche, ED 111
     222. The author defines and discusses the linguistic phenomenon of
code-switching. Many teachers of Mexican American pupils do not understand
why some bilingual pupils switch from one code to another. For the educator
and bilingual education consultant interested in understanding the causes of
language-switching.

497. RAMÍREZ, María Irene. "A Comparison of Three Methods of Teaching
     the Spanish-Speaking Student. " Unpublished Doctoral Dissertation, East
     Texas State University, 1971. In this outstanding educational study, the
researcher emphasizes that an ideal bilingual program is one in which all of
the students are taught in both languages throughout the school day for the dura-
tion of the school year. However, the researcher is quick to point out that there
may be variations in a bilingual program. For example, some subjects may be
taught bilingually while other subjects may not.

498. SUMMER BILINGUAL INSTITUTE. "Bilingual Elementary Schooling:
        A Report to Texas Educators," Summer Bilingual Institute at Univer-
        sity of Texas, Austin, Texas,1968. ERIC Microfiche ED 026 919. Ele-
mentary school teachers in a bilingual classroom who want to better understand the educational problems of their Mexican American pupils will want to
refer to this publication. Educational problems and solutions are discussed.

499. TEXAS EDUCATION AGENCY. Proceedings of the First Texas Con-
        ference for the Mexican-American. Held in San Antonio, Texas, April
        13-15, 1967. Edited by Dwain M. Estes. Austin, Texas: The Agency,
1967. This publication lists many of the educational problems of Mexican
American students in Texas. An important document for scholars interested
in doing research on the Mexican American student.

500. UNITED STATES COMMISSION ON CIVIL RIGHTS. A Better Chance
        to Learn: Bilingual/Bicultural Education. Washington, D.C.: Govern-
        ment Printing Office, 1974. A federal government report on the virtues
of bilingual-bicultural education which should be of special interest to central
office school administrators whose districts have a faltering bilingual education program.

501. _____. Mexican-American Education Study, Report I: Ethnic Isolation
        of Mexican-Americans in the Public Schools of the Southwest. Washing-
        ton, D.C.: United States Government Printing Office, 1971. A federal
government educational report on the status of public school education for
Mexican American students in California, Texas, Arizona, New Mexico, and
Colorado.

502. _____. The Unfinished Education, Mexican-American Educational
        Series, Report II. Washington, D.C.: United States Government Print-
        ing Office, 1971. This federal government educational report concludes
that all is not well for Mexican American students in our nation's public schools.
Unsolved educational problems are listed.

503. WASHINGTON, David E. "Cultural Pluralism: Are Teachers Prepared?"
        Phi Delta Kappan, Volume 63, No. 7 (March 1982), pages 493-495. This
        piece is filled with information and statistics about American colleges and
universities that offer bilingual-bicultural education programs. Of 3,038 institutions surveyed, 241 institutions offered a bilingual-bicultural program and
135 institutions offered a multicultural program. Forty different languages
are taught in the various bilingual-bicultural programs in the United States.
This piece should prove enlightening to the educational researcher who needs
basic statistics on the status of American bilingual-bicultural education and
American multicultural education.

504. WILSON, Herbert B. "Evaluation of the Influence of Educational Programs
        on Mexican Americans," 1968. ERIC Microfiche, ED 016 561. This
        study was conducted to determine which factors contribute to the educa-
tional retardation of some Mexican American pupils.

XI

REFERENCES, TEXTBOOKS,
AND BIBLIOGRAPHIES

Many university students taking courses in bilingual-bicultural education frequently are asked by their professors to prepare research projects and term papers on various aspects of bilingual-bicultural education. Before a student begins preparing a formal paper for a professor, he or she usually has to refer to a number of textbooks, sourcebooks, and bibliographies. The sources in this section should prove useful to a student in the initial preparation of a paper.

The sources in this section also should be beneficial to professors, school administrators, teachers, consultants and scholars who want to gain additional insights into bilingualism, bilingual-bicultural education, multicultural education and the Hispanic culture.

This section contains the following types of works: (a) sourcebooks, (b) handbooks, (c) bibliographies, (d) essay collections, (e) collections of readings, (f) foreign language textbooks, (g) English as a second language textbooks, (h) bilingual-bicultural education readers, (i) dual language dictionaries, (j) academic dictionaries, and (k) staff development reference books.

505. ALBERT, Martin L., and L. K. Obler. The Bilingual Brain: Neuropsychological and Neurolinguistic Aspects of Bilingualism. New York: Academic Press, 1978. This work answers technical questions concerning the psychological, neurological, and linguistic aspects of speaking two languages.

506. ALTUS, David M. "Mexican American Education, A Selected Bibliography," 1971. ERIC Microfiche, ED 048 961. This work is for the bilingual-bicultural education major who is preparing a term paper on the education of disadvantaged Mexican American school children.

507. BABIN, Patrick. "Bilingualism: A Bibliography," 1968. ERIC Microfiche ED 032 097. This is a selected bibliography of bibliographies, books, unpublished papers, articles and books on bilingualism.

508. BANKS, James A. (editor). Education in the 80's: Multiethnic Education. Washington, D.C.: National Education Association, 1981. This is a collection of fourteen essays which were written by seventeen essay contributors. A well-organized book which should prove useful as a basic multicultural education reader at the university level. Length: 190 pages.

509. _____. Multiethnic Education: Practices and Promises. Bloomington, Indiana: Phi Delta Kappa, 1976. Multiethnic education is an education that provides for the linguistic, cultural, and psychological needs of all students, regardless of their ethnic group membership. Banks' publication delves into the intricacies and rewards of this form of education.

510. BAPTISTE, H. Prentice. Multicultural Education: A Synopsis. Washington, D.C.: University Press of America, 1979. A collection of essays by experts in multicultural education and bilingual education. Length: 209 pages.

511. _____. , and M. L. Baptiste. Developing the Multicultural Process in Classroom Instruction: Competencies for Teachers. Washington, D.C.: University Press of America, 1979. This book provides administrators and teachers with current field-tested competencies in the field of multicultural education. Length: 286 pages.

512. BARKER, Marie E. Español para el Bilingüe. Skokie, Illinois: National Textbook Company, 1973. A book for instructors who teach the Spanish language to Spanish-English bilingual students.

513. CASTILLO, Carlos, and Otto F. Bond. The University of Chicago Spanish-English, English-Spanish Dictionary. New York: Washington Square Press, 1971. A paperback mass market dictionary especially recommended for college level Spanish majors and for Spanish teachers at the secondary school level.

514. COHEN, S. Alan. Teach Them All to Read. New York: Random House, 1969. All children of normal intelligence who do not have a learning disability can be taught to read if the proper motivational foundation can be laid by both parents and teachers. An excellent book for the bilingual program reading specialist who constantly is being asked to solve student reading problems.

515. COLANGELO, Nicholas, and C. H. Foxley (editors). Multicultural Nonsexist Education: A Human Relations Approach. Dubuque, Iowa: Kendall/Hunt Publishing Company, 1979. This book of readings about multicultural education, nonsexist education, social change and bilingual education can be utilized as a staff development textbook. Softcover. Length: 416 pages.

516. CORDASCO, Francesco. Bilingual Education in American Schools: A Guide to Information Sources. Detroit: Gale Research Company, 1979. This partially annotated bibliography on American bilingual education should prove useful to university students working on term papers on bilingualism. University professors can use this reference work in their preparation of class lectures. The material is organized into nine headings.

517. _____. Bilingual Schooling in the United States: A Sourcebook for Educational Personnel. New York: McGraw Hill, 1976. An invaluable book of readings for school administrators and teachers assigned to a bilingual education program. Length: 387 pages.

518. CROSS, Dolores E., and G. C. Baker (editors). Teaching in a Multicultural Society: Perspectives and Professional Strategies. New York: The Free Press, 1977. This publication is a collection of twelve essays written by various contributors which can be used as an introductory bicultural or multicultural education textbook.

519. DE LEON, Fidel. Español: Material Para El Hispano. Manchaca, Texas: Sterling Swift Publishing Company, 1978. This text contains Spanish language lessons for the Hispanic student's first year of college level Spanish. Soft cover.

520. DIXSON, Robert J. Complete Course in English. New York: Regents
     publishing Company, 1977. For the Spanish-dominant bilingual teacher
     aide who is serious about improving her/his English language proficien-
cy.

521. DURÁN, Livie I. (editor). Introduction to Chicano Studies. New York:
     MacMillan Publishing Company, 1973. Most educators do not realize
     that the American bilingual education movement and the Chicano move-
ment are interrelated social phenomena. Durán's book is one of the better
introductory works on Chicano studies. High school teachers and college professors of Chicano studies will want to review this text.

522. FISHMAN, Joshua A. Bilingual Education: An International Sociological
     Perspective. Rowley, Massachusetts: Newbury House, 1976. For the
     professor of bilingual education who is searching for a book which dis-
cusses international bilingual education. Too many bilingual education books
discuss bilingual education only as it exists in certain sections of the nation.
Fishman's text gives the reader an international overview of the subject.

523. FUENTES, Dagoberto, and José A. López. Barrio Language Dictionary:
     First Dictionary of Calo. La Puente, California: Sunburst Enterprises,
     1977. P. O. Box 391, zip code 91747. Mexican Americans have long
realized that some members of their ethnic group speak a form of the Spanish
language which is not exactly a standard dialect of Spanish. Spanish language
majors and linguists will be amused and perhaps fascinated by some of the
terms in this Chicano Spanish dictionary.

524. GAARDER, A. B. Bilingual Schooling and the Survival of Spanish in the
     United States. Rowley, Massachusetts: Newbury House, 1977. The author
     contends that bilingual education is one way of insuring that the Spanish
language will not disappear in the United States. A book filled with insights
into American bilingual education which is recommended reading for college
students majoring in bilingual-bicultural education.

525. GALVAN, Roberto A., and R. V. Teschner. El diccionario del español
     chicano. Silver Spring, Maryland: Institute of Modern Languages, Inc.,
     1977. Many Mexican Americans speak a distinctive form of the Spanish
language. Some linguists refer to the Mexican American's Spanish as "Chicano
Spanish." This dictionary acquaints the reader with the vocabulary of Chicano
Spanish.

526. GOLD, Milton J. (editor). In Praise of Diversity: A Resource Book for
     Multicultural Education. Washington, D.C.: Teacher Corps, 1977.
     This book of readings espouses the belief that ethnic diversity is bene-
ficial, wholesome, and beautiful.

527. GRAY, Tracy C. The Current Status of Bilingual Education Legislation:
     An Update. Washington, D.C.: The Center for Applied Linguistics,
     1981. This publication contains the important U.S. Supreme Court
decisions and federal legislation which affect foreign language learning and
the bilingual instruction of children. Also listed are the statutory and consti-
tutional provisions of each of the American states which affect the bilingual-
bicultural education of children. Length: 105 pages.

528. HERRERA, Diane (editor). Puerto Ricans and Other Minority Groups
     in the Continental United States: An Annotated Bibliography. Second
     Edition. Detroit: Blaine Ethridge, 1979. This work is almost a duplicate

of the material available twice in Eric Microfiche ED 104 983 and ED 108 488. Nevertheless, this bibliography contains many elusive sources which should be of interest to graduate students and professionals in education. Length: 397 pages.

529. HILLSON, Maurie, and Joseph Bongo. Continuous-Progress Educa-
      tion: A Practical Approach. Palo Alto, California: Science Research
      Associates, 1971. The authors of this text maintain that although na-
tive speakers of English profit greatly from continuous-progress, nongraded
education, this form of education is highly beneficial for non-English-speaking children who must master English in addition to the academic knowledge
and skills usually assimilated by their school peers.

530. HOPKINS, Lee Bennett. Let Them Be Themselves. New York: Ci-
      tation Press, 1974. Many teachers cause their students to behave in
      ways that are incompatible with their personality or with their up-
bringing. Too often, students begin to behave in ways that will let them sur-
vive in the classroom. Hopkins has written a book which will help educators
help students to be themselves. Suggested reading for teachers in pluralistic
schools.

531. IBARRA, Herb. "Bibliography of ESL/Bilingual Teaching Materials,"
      1969. San Diego City Schools, California, ERIC Microfiche ED 028
      002. Four hundred and six sources for ESL and bilingual education
teachers are listed in this book of sources published between 1945 and 1968.

532. JORDAN, L. B. Mexican Americans: Resources to Build Cultural
      Understanding. Littleton, Colorado: Libraries Unlimited, Inc. , 1973.
      This publication describes book and nonbook materials.

533. LA FONTAINE, Hernan (editor). Bilingual Education. Wayne, New
      Jersey: Avery Publishing Group, Inc. , 1978. One of the more popular
      bilingual education texts on the market. A valuable reference book for
professors of bilingual education.

534. LAMBERT, Wallace E. , and G. R. Tucker. The Bilingual Education of
      Children. Rowley, Massachusetts: Newbury House, 1971. This work
      provides a logical rationale for bilingual education. A basic text which
is recommended reading for college students majoring in bilingual education.

535. LINSKIE, Rosella, and Howard Rosenberg. A Handbook for Multicult-
      ural Studies in Elementary Schools, Book I: Chicano, Black, Asian
      and Native Americans. San Francisco: R&E Research Associates,
1978. Each student wants to know that members of his ethnic group have
made contributions to the history and development of their nation. Too many
school textbooks omit the social contributions of some American ethnic
groups. The authors discuss the importance of including the social contributions of American minority groups in the elementary school curriculum.

536. LISMORE, Thomas. Welcome to English. New York: Regents Pub-
      lishing Company, 1977. Regents Publishing Company specializes in
      ESL (English as a Second Language) textbooks and Lismore's book is
one of the best on the market. Recommended for the foreign student in the
United States wishing to master the English language quickly.

537. MACKEY, W. F. Bilingual Education in a Binational School. Rowley, Massachusetts: Newbury House, 1971. This work has a philosophical orientation and should appeal to professors of bilingual education.

538. MCHENRY, J. Patrick. A Short History of Mexico. Garden City, New York: Doubleday and Company, 1970. Historians who specialize in Latin American history will want to make this work available to their history students. This text can be used as a high school social studies reference book in an English-Spanish bicultural classroom.

539. NEWMARK, Maxim. Dictionary of Spanish Literature. New Jersey: Littlefield, Adams & Company, 1965. An excellent, convenient reference work for American students of Spanish and Spanish American literature. This work also can be used as a literature reference book in a high school with a multicultural literature course. The treatment is objective, factual, and concise. Included are Spanish and Latin American poets, novelists, essayists, dramatists, and literary critics. Length: 352 pages. Soft cover.

540. PAREDES, Americo. Mexican-American Authors. Boston: Houghton Mifflin Company, 1972. Paredes has a national reputation as a scholar and as a writer of books about the Mexican American. This book is for the person interested in reading about authors of Mexican American descent and can be used as a reference work in an English-Spanish bicultural literature class at the high school level.

541. PITTARO, John M. , and Alexander Green. Primer Curso Para Todos. Boston: D.C. Heath & Company, 1959. A first-year Spanish language textbook. This 492-page hardcover book may be used at the high school or junior college level.

542. POSTON, Lawrence, and Eugenio Chang-Rodrigues. Continuing Spanish II. New York: American Book Company, 1967. A 367-page hardcover college level Spanish language textbook which was a project of the Modern Language Association.

543. QUIRARTE, Jacinto. Mexican American Artists. Austin, Texas: University of Texas Press, 1973. Residents of the Southwest are aware that the Mexican American culture has produced a large number of highly talented artists. Quirarte, a University of Texas professor, has penned a book which will familiarize the reader with the Mexican American community's contributions to the field of art. An appropriate book for high school libraries which serve an English-Spanish bilingual education program.

544. REILLY, Robert P. A Selected and Annotated Bibliography of Bicultural Classroom Materials for Mexican American Studies. San Francisco: R&E Research Associates, 1977. For the harassed Mexican American studies instructor who can never seem to find appropriate materials for his students. Soft cover.

545. RIVERA, Feliciano. A Mexican American Source Book with Study Guideline. Menlo Park, California: Educational Consulting Associates, 1970. This work can be used by: (a) the Mexican American studies teacher, (b) the ethnic studies instructor, and (c) the secondary bilingual classroom teacher of Mexican Americans.

546. ROLLINS, Joan (editor). Hidden Minorities: The Persistence of
     Ethnicity in American Life. Washington, D.C.: University Press
     of America, 1982. Recommended reading for the teacher who teaches
in an "ethnic school." Anyone who wants to become more familiar with
American ethnic groups will find value in this publication.

547. SANTAMARIA, Francisco J. Diccionario De Mejicanismos. Mexico
     City, Mexico: Editorial Porrua, S. A., 1974. This is a collection
     of "Mexicanisms," Spanish language words which originated in Mexico.
This hardcover work was published in Mexico and written in Spanish. For
the graduate student of bilingual-bicultural education.

548. SAVILLE, Muriel, and Rudolph Troike. "Handbook of Bilingual Edu-
     cation," 1970. ERIC Microfiche, ED 035 465. School administrators,
     especially directors of bilingual education, will want to familiarize
themselves with the content of this handbook. Both Saville and Troike are
nationally known bilingual education experts and their publication is recommended reading for all university students majoring in bilingual-bicultural
education.

549. SIMS, William E., and Bernice Bass De Martinez. Perspectives in
     Multicultural Education. Washington, D.C.: University Press of
     America, 1981. Discussed are the factors which constitute an effec-
tive multicultural education. For the teacher of culturally diverse learners.
Length: 230 pages.

550. STONE, James C., and Donald P. De Nevi. Teaching Multicultural
     Populations -- Five Heritages. New York: Van Nostrand Reinhold
     Company, 1971. The authors discuss the problems and challenges
which are part of teaching Americans of Mexican, Puerto Rican, Indian,
African, and Asian ancestry. One of the better texts on multicultural education which can be used as an introductory educational sociology text.

551. STUPP, Emma G., and Jennifer Gage. A Bibliography on Bilingual
     Teachers: Competencies, Certification, and Training. Rosslyn,
     Virginia: National Clearinghouse for Bilingual Education, 1981. This
is a collection of nearly forty entries with full abstracts concerning degree
requirements, employment patterns, credentials, and placement of bilingual
teachers, Length: 34 pages.

552. SULLIVAN, Edward C. Speak English Now. New York: College Skills
     Center, 1975. A practical book for the American immigrant or the
     foreign student in the United States who wants to master the English
language posthaste.

553. TROIKE, R. C. Research Evidence for the Effectiveness of Bilingual
     Education. Rosslyn, Virginia: Center for Applied Linguistics, 1978.
     Recommended reading for the individual not convinced about the effec-
tiveness of American bilingual education programs.

554. TRUEBA, Henry T. Bilingual Bicultural Education for the Spanish
     Speaking in the United States. Champaign, Illinois: Stipes Publishing
     Company, 1977. Graduate and doctoral students majoring in linguistics
and bilingual education will want to refer to this publication before taking
their written exams.

555. VON MALTITZ, Frances Willard. Living and Learning in Two Languages: Bilingual-Bicultural Education in the United States. New York McGraw-Hill Book Company, 1975. This book contains a history of bilingual education in the United States. A quality hardcover book which can be used as a textbook in an introductory bilingual education course.

556. WILLIAMS, Frederick   (editor). Language and Poverty. Chicago: Markham Publishing Company, 1971. A collection of material on verbal language and the effect that poverty has on a person's language. For the sociolinguistically inclined bilingual education specialist.